STONE
SECRETS

Best wishes
Medina F. Saleh

Other works by Mediha F. Saliba

Nonfiction—
SHADOWS OF THE PUPPET

STONE SECRETS

A PERSONAL JOURNEY

AS GATHERED FROM THE STORIES
OF ESPERALDA (DEE) HERFKINS

MEDIHA F. SALIBA

STONEPEOPLE'S PRESS
TARZANA, CALIFORNIA

StonePeople's Press
5035 Bilmoor Avenue
Tarzana, CA 91356

ISBN: 0-9675635-0-X

For Gina and Jeff—

so they may understand their mother,
and to remind others with painful,
haunting memories
that stories release.

Foreword

"I HAVE A story to tell," my Aunt Dee told me on the phone one day. "Something I have to say now that your Uncle Harry has passed away. You're a nurse. You'll understand."

Would I listen?

Of course. But when I accepted my aunt's invitation to meet with her and listen to her story, I didn't realize what I was getting into. I had no idea of the horrors she had endured during her younger years, nor did I know of the pain she lived with daily.

For more than a decade Aunt Dee had suffered with the debilitating illness, but she bore her pain quietly. We, in her extended family, knew she had arthritis but thought it was under control. Why should we think otherwise? Aunt Dee always wore a smile, said she was fine.

As Aunt Dee told her story over the next fourteen months, I could barely keep my own body from becoming stiff with the tension of cruelty, helplessness, and loss. Her past spoke of secrets she had kept to herself until they had hardened and crystallized like polished amber, locking life inside. Her present spoke of pain and confusion, and heavy doses of medication that she described as ripping at her stomach. Her life had become a *non*life. She needed and wanted help.

My journey with her became threefold: To listen to her stories without judgment. To write the stories as she told them to me. To offer understanding and healing through the mapping of her life's patterns. The rest of what happened came as a surprise to both of us.

Stones

What is a stone?
A piece of rock?
A giant bluff?
A wall to hide behind?
Feelings trapped in cold
      gray
              darkness?
In medicine
      a stone is something inflexible and
rounded
      causing dis-ease
          sickness
              and pain.
In life
      it is an impurity
          gnawing
              at the soul.
A cover grown hard
to protect
the inner jewel,
the precious gem that
waits
inside
to be
recognized.

Introduction

HEALING IS A curious business. Too often I've seen people who repress their feelings and memories, hold back images of pain, lock the past away. These are the people who guard their fear and anger, smile and pretend nothing is wrong. But at night, when one swims in the unconscious of the soul, these fears come like ghosts, haunting, pressing in, until illness presses out. In Dee Herfkins' case the ghosts came breathing fire, turning her joints into molten red, then hardened, stone.

Dee had locked away a lifetime of childhood nightmares, war atrocities, death, and the feelings of hopelessness and helplessness that came with them. In 1985, as if prophesying her own life, she told her husband, "My feet hurt all the time. I can't walk in my shoes." On the physical plane she was describing her need for bunion surgery, a procedure that frightened her beyond the scope of most people. Viewed in archetypal metaphor, she was describing her inability to walk further along her life's path in the same shoes.

The anxiety about her surgery, coupled with her grown daughter's disturbing lifestyle, triggered in Dee a series of symptoms that would later be diagnosed as rheumatoid arthritis. All at once, she was thrown into the pits of hell, the dark night of the soul. For the next twelve years physical pain wracked her body. Allopathic medication helped control the pain but offered nothing for Dee's mind and spirit. Heavy doses of medication often left her nauseated and weak and in some cases, led to bleeding of the gums and stomach ulcers.

As the years of physical pain continued, Dee became more and more open to alternatives—anything. Although she continued with her standard medication, she experimented with massage, chelation, removal of mercury tooth fillings, and other practices. Not until *Ayurveda* (an East Indian form of medicine) and homeopathy, did she begin to feel results; a better sense of well-being and finally, a need to express. Her expression first took the form of painting. Then she wanted someone to talk to. Someone she could trust, and who would listen to her stories.

I became that listener.

Dee remained remarkably stoic as she related her stories to me. Occasionally there was a tear, a sniffle, a tremble of her lips and jaw, but mostly her face remained expressionless, and her body rigid and erect.

As a nurse for more than twenty-five years, it did not take me long to discover that I needed a broader base in my understanding of rheumatoid arthritis. I contacted the medical library to help me unearth anything new in the area of rheumatology. Classic definitions describe the illness as a systemic immunological disease characterized by joint inflammation. Causes are vague, pointing to stress and feelings of hopelessness and helplessness. Treatments have improved, but the goal of a cure remains unrealistic.

Not very encouraging. I dug deeper, searching the journals of alternative medicine, psychology, and psychiatry. According to psychiatrist Dr. Jambur Ananth, arthritis immune processes are related to psychological events. This concept piqued my interest, but what were the criteria of a psychological event?

In Ayurveda, rheumatoid arthritis is considered a multilayered illness. Dr. David Frawley, head of the American Institute of Vedic Studies, states, "real emotional nourishment comes from within as the power of love. We cannot simply pick it up from the outside like we can good food, though as children, when our inner connections are not entirely formed, we require love from the outside to sustain us."

Dr. Clarissa Pinkola Estés, psychologist and beloved cantadora (storyteller), speaks of archetypes and fairy tales that often depict the loss of innocence. "There is nothing worse than the person who has lost their innocence leaving nothing to take its place," she said in one of her lectures. "This then becomes the person who is prey to all inner and outer predators."

Could we not take predators to also mean illness? And if so, could we not expel that predator by shining a light?

Traditional medicine believes that disease has a

course. There is a time of onset, a climax, and then a resolution—either cure, remission, or death. What has been left out is how the patient handles his/her illness, or even why the patient has contracted the illness to begin with. Past experiences and hardships survived can be just as important as a medical history. The truths of memories have always been suspect. Does an adult really accurately remember events that happened when he or she was four? What a mind *believes* to have happened is the issue. That "truth" has the potential to act on the body at the cellular level.

Listening to life-stories helps shine a light, mapping unconscious patterns that have repeated and repeated without allowing the conscious mind to successfully process and resolve them. It is not only important to tell the stories, but also to write and especially, REREAD them, for it is in this process of reading your life in story form that healing occurs.

STONE SECRETS

A PERSONAL JOURNEY

Larimar

Larimar is blue
and sings the song of freedom,
no cage can hold prisoner
the spirit that spreads its wings
and finds courage in the quest
to experience
feelings.

One

March 1997

"I'M SO GLAD you could come," Aunt Dee said, her voice soft like a child, but formal and uncertain, her heavy Dutch accent laced with a quiver.

She stood in the open doorway looking just as she always did. Her hair, tinted a natural black, hung in soft waves to her shoulders, framing a pale, ivory-skinned face. Her lips, painted deep red, wore a wide, but somehow expressionless, smile. And her eyes. Those hazel eyes, were as I always remembered them, dull, as if locked in another place and time. But now, as they did when I was younger, they had a way of drawing me in, pulling me into a pool of some hidden emotion.

I smiled back and bent over to hug her tiny, five-feet-at-best frame. She felt frail, almost breakable in my embrace. Of course I'd come. She had sounded so mysterious, even desperate, when she'd phoned.

With deformed fingers that could no longer bend, she motioned me to the living room and led the way, hobbling in stocking feet. I quickly removed my own shoes, left them neatly by the door, and followed her.

Aunt Dee sat down on the couch, offering me the seat beside her. She drew in a slow, deep breath, exhaled, then told me that Uncle Harry's recent passing had brought up her pain and fear from the past. She needed to talk to someone. Someone who would understand. She didn't want to die without telling her children her story, without her children knowing what her life had been like.

"I wanted to write my own story." She held out her hands. "But I can't write. I have to put my hands under hot running water when they become too painful, so I've never gotten further than this." She took a frayed folder from the coffee table and handed me ten pages of large, shaky print. She looked at me with the eyes of an innocent child. "You're a nurse. You're a writer. Help me . . ." She rubbed her hands together, looked down at the papers in my hand. "Last month when Harry died, there was a moment when I thought the world would end. I was so afraid of being alone."

"You're not alone," I reminded her gently. "You have your two children. Gina has a husband and a son. Jeff has a wife. They are all your family."

"Yes, I know," she said, looking back up at me. "They took care of me when their father died. I love them so much. I want them to know I need them. I want them to understand why they are so important to me."

Her gaze dropped again to the pages in my hand. I glanced at the one on top. It began: "To a child, any child, a family is so important, a warm loving family . . ." I scanned a few more pages, read the last one. She wrote of good memories she wanted her children and grandson to know about. She began with the importance of family, and how wonderful and loving her father and mother were. In a distant and formal writing style, she described her mother as beautiful, with soft, pale skin, dark hair, and green eyes. Her father was the prince; he was caring, strong-willed, and full of faith, a minister as well as a musician. She told of little carved boats, and walks in flower gardens.

Her opening page reminded me of the beginning of any fairy tale—all is well in Paradise. But quickly, the good memories fell away and were replaced with tales of war, Japanese camps, and death.

I took a deep breath and laid the papers back on the table. I knew that between the lines of her written pages were ghosts that haunted her, images and memories she wanted to forget.

I took my aunt's hands. They were swollen and red. She flinched slightly, as though afraid of my touch. I looked into her face. With the gift of my own maturity I began to see my aunt more clearly. A

3

denseness hung about her like dark, heavy vapor. Her eyes were pools of trapped shadows, and her mouth, though turned up in a smile, held something back. Sorrow perhaps—a sadness lingered in the corners. Her lips trembled. Imprisoned feelings wanting freedom? I looked back down at her hands.

"How long has it been?" I asked.

"This?" She withdrew her hands from mine. "This, since 1985, but . . ." She paused, thinking, weighing something in her mind. She gazed at her hands, at some imaginary thing in front of her. "It really started much earlier. 1959. I was twenty-five when we fled to the Netherlands from Indonesia. We were so happy to escape, but still, Java had been our home. I missed the warm tropical air, the wide-open spaces, and fields and fields of rice paddies. Everything so green. Holland was very different, cold and wet. The houses were built one next to the other and on top of each other." She shivered just thinking of it. "The government housing we were given consisted of one room. Seven of us shared that room: your Uncle Harry, me, my daughter Gina, almost three, Harry's mother, brother, sister, and a few months later Jeff, my son.

"Those were difficult times," she said. "Harry worked long hours learning European car mechanics. His sister went to school. His brother was in the Dutch military. I was pregnant with Jeff. I stayed home with Sitie Katminah, Harry's mother, and helped her with things around the house, cleaning, shopping, cooking.

"Amidst the confusion of trying to get used to another culture, Gina became sick with a kidney infection. Oh how she cried when she urinated.

Blood streaked the yellow gold. Frightened, I quickly took her to the doctor, but still she cried.

"'Give her some of this to drink,' Sitie Katminah told me. 'It will help her.'

'What is it?' I asked, looking at the dark brew my mother-in-law had cooked up.

"'It's a tea made from herbs. It will help cleanse her.'

"'The doctor already gave me antibiotics,' I said.

"Sitie Katminah nodded her head but pressed the cup of tea into my hands. 'Let her try this too.'

"I didn't want to leave any stone unturned when it came to the health of my child. I offered her the tea. A cup then, a cup later, and the next day, and the next. The blood in Gina's urine cleared, and she quit crying. I didn't know whether it was the antibiotics or the tea. It didn't matter, as long as my baby was well again."

As Aunt Dee explained to me, her days went by in a comfortable routine, and her pregnancy remained uneventful. When she went into labor, Harry took her to the hospital. With some difficulty, but no complications, she delivered a healthy baby boy.

"A boy! A son for Harry." She smiled at me. Her eyes showed a flicker of joy, but it quickly disappeared back into blue gray shadows.

"Jeff was only a couple months old when I became sick with strep throat. Within two weeks my whole body ached, and I couldn't move or bend my fingers. I couldn't lift Jeff to take care of him. It frightened me. I didn't know what was happening to me.

"Harry took me to the doctor. The next thing I knew, I was in the hospital. Jeff came with me. I'm not sure why. Perhaps because the Dutch do not like to separate a mother and infant, or maybe they were observing him for symptoms. I don't know. We were kept in isolation, and the family could only wave to us through the glass window. For six weeks they treated me with shots and bed rest, while the nurses cared for Jeff.

"I left the hospital feeling better, but I never fully recovered. Cold, icy feelings would wash over me, creep into my bones, leave me weak and in need of rest. But time passed, and I didn't give too much thought to my occasional weak spells or my sensitivity to cold. I believed they were a part of my recovery. They would pass, and they did. Then, in 1985, more than twenty-five years later, the symptoms returned with a vengeance."

Aunt Dee looked down at her hands. Several times she opened her mouth to speak but changed her mind. Finally, she stood up and said, "Let me get you something to drink."

"Don't trouble yourself," I started to say, but she was already moving over the plastic runner that followed the length of the pale blue carpet from the kitchen to the sliding glass door leading to the backyard. As she disappeared into the kitchen I got up and walked along the runner to look outside. Neat and well-manicured, the yard reminded me of the gardens in fairytale books. Past the edge of the patio, a strip of hillside was covered with myrtle and trailing rosemary. A small peach tree hung heavy with fruit. Perfectly round white peaches with a blush of pink promised sweetness when ripe. Tiny trimmed bushes, with splashes of purple violets in-between, lined the walkway to a gated swimming pool. On the ground just outside the glass door, on a flowered plastic place mat, were two tiny bowls. One had water, the other dry kibble.

"You have a cat? Or a little dog?" I called to my aunt, still busy in the kitchen.

"Cat," she called back. "I don't like dogs. They scare me, and they're messy."

I glanced again around the yard. A cat made sense. There were no trampled shrubs, no pounded paths where a dog might run back and forth barking at neighbors or passersby, no brown piles on the cement or grass. All lay neat and tidy, nothing overgrown, no scattered leaves across the patio, no extra frills. Simple, like her living room—no clutter and everything in its place.

The living room walls were bare except for one painting that hung next to the couch; in it, a full moon cast a shaft of light on a lone sailboat crossing a dark sea. The painting made me sad. The whole house suddenly felt sad. Even the gentle piano music playing on the stereo seemed to weep. Perhaps I felt my aunt's loneliness. Uncle Harry had been gone less than a month.

I walked to the china cabinet in the corner. There were pictures of Aunt Dee's children, their spouses, and her one grandson. There was a picture of Dee's mother and father, and one of Uncle Harry's mother and father. Oddly, there were none of Dee or Harry. As I pondered this absence, my gaze was drawn to the side of the cabinet. Propped against the wall, partially hidden by the cabinet, were three unframed paintings. I pulled them out to take a peek. Done in acrylic, the heavy strokes, dark and bold, screamed out at me. What exactly they screamed, I wasn't sure.

"You paint?" I called again over the low partition to the kitchen.

"Well ... yes, I guess so. Gina thought it might be good for me."

I know little of painting, though I found Aunt Dee's art had its appeal. One of them, probably her first, was of pinkish orange flowers. They lay on the canvas, dark centers gaping as if caught in a nightmarish cry. The composition with purple irises had more light. Placed in a round vase, the bold strokes in the flowers had been pacified with leaves and graceful ferns. The third painting, a nighttime seascape, had a sense of movement; stormy sky, angry waves, and wind. All three paintings reflected a sadness in their dark tones, a solemnity, yet also a reverence.

"Here we go." Aunt Dee hobbled around the kitchen counter with a tall glass of orange juice poised between both hands, her fingers sticking rigidly out beyond the moist curves of the glass.

I crossed the small living room to take the glass from her and placed it on a cork coaster, on the table.

"I've only been painting a few months," she said, wiping the moisture from her fingers by massaging her hands together. "I started a couple of weeks before Harry's heart attack. I'm not very good," she apologized. "But Harry liked what I did, and Gina and Jeff continue to encourage me. I can't work for long periods of time. These fingers." She looked at her hands. "They are so, so ... I used to have such beautiful hands," she said, rubbing her joints. "I used to dance you know. The *Serimpi, Tari Sampur, Tari Topeng*." She named the Indonesian temple dances as her eyes took on a faraway look.

She walked to the fireplace and pointed out a picture on the narrow mantel. I hadn't noticed it before. The black and white photograph was slightly faded, but I could clearly see my aunt as a young woman dressed in the traditional costume of an Indonesian temple dancer: the *lereng* print batik and small-strapped top, the beaded armbands and head-piece, and the soft scarves that billowed at the waist.

"It's a beautiful costume," I said, picking up the picture to look at it more closely.

"Harry made it for me."

I stared back at her, surprised. I only knew my uncle as a mechanic, one of the best foreign-car mechanics in our area. According to my mother, that was how Aunt Dee and Uncle Harry got their immi-gration papers so quickly. Men with his expertise were needed in the United States in the 1960s—a time of growing Mercedes and BMW imports, VW Bugs, and VW Buses. Foreign-car mechanics were in demand. Everyone I knew went to Uncle Harry, but—a seamster?

"Your uncle made all my costumes. He spent hours on the beadwork. He loved that I danced . . . then."

She hesitated, took the photograph from my hands.

"I was quite good," she said shyly. Then she fell silent. She continued to examine the photograph.

I could sense her groping through the dark caves of her memories.

"In Indonesia," she began slowly, "I danced at many different affairs, but something happened one day that made me question whether I, as a Christian, should be doing these temple dances. My teacher gave me a carved *kris* [dagger] and told me I should wear it during our next performance. 'It will be your guide,' he told me. 'You will dance better than ever.' This frightened me. I knew there were strange forms of magic among the native people. We lived in Central Java where the most famous dagger makers lived. I had heard stories of daggers that flew on their own through the sky, daggers that had their own personality and protected their masters, daggers that glowed green when touched. There were all kinds of frightening stories. I didn't want any part of that native magic. I was a good Christian.

"I refused to wear the dagger, and that started me wondering about my dancing. Should I be doing these spirit dances? What kind of evilness might I bring upon myself? After that I danced less and less, until I gave it up altogether."

"And what did Uncle Harry think of you giving it up?"

"He agreed."

"But all those costumes. What did you do with them?"

Aunt Dee placed the picture back on the mantel, walked around the coffee table, and lowered herself onto the couch. She crossed her hands in her lap.

"I burned them. When we came to the United States, I wanted to start my new life pure. Harry and I made a fire in the backyard and we burned them. All of them. I even burned all the pictures of me dancing. That one is the only one left. I don't know how it survived. Maybe Gina hid it."

She left me speechless. I, too, had danced those dances as a young teenager here in the United States. My mother had nearly gone blind sewing beads and sequins, and to this day I still have the few costumes she made. I love them for the energy she put into them, for their beauty, for the connection to my roots. I never thought of them as having any powers related to black magic. Nor did my parents or I feel we were violating our faith by dancing the dances of the Indonesian temples. The dances belonged to a time when Hinduism and Buddhism became Javanized. To us, the dances and their costumes were a part of our heritage, part of our Indonesian culture, and had nothing to do with religion.

I wondered what could possibly have gone on in my aunt's life that she should feel so heavily burdened by superstition. Why did she have the need to burn her past, the need to purify herself?

I glanced again at the picture on the mantel. An angelic face stared back from a time before I was born. Graceful hands held the fine cloth of her costume. But the eyes. The eyes already kept something veiled.

As I moved to join her on the couch, my gaze fell once again upon the midnight seascape, and I thought she might have painted that as well. The sadness and the gray tones matched hers, but the strokes felt softer.

"No, I didn't paint that," she answered, when I asked. "That's a picture Harry and I picked out long ago, when we first arrived in the United States."

She and Uncle Harry must have felt very alone when first coming to this new world. Immigration is not as easy or romantic as Hollywood portrays.

"You must miss Indonesia?"

"Oh no. I never want to go back," Aunt Dee whispered, moving both her stiff hands in slow, almost dancelike movements across her face. Her gaze drifted down to her handwritten pages on the table. "I don't have many good memories." She paused for an instant. "My family were good Christians. My father was a minister. I loved listening to him speak in church. From an early age he taught us to love God." Her eyes softened to some distant image. For a moment she seemed to float on a sweet memory. Then I felt her mind settle elsewhere. "Most memories . . ." She shook her head, looked me square in the face. "Most of my memories are not good. In Indonesia there are strange things. Forces. Unexplainable forces. Ungodly forces."

She took a deep breath and lowered her head. She traced the veins of one hand with the index finger of the other. After another deep breath and, without looking up, she began.

"When Harry and I were first married, we lived with his mother, Sitie Katminah, and his younger brother and sister. His father died just after the war—complications from life in the Japanese camps. Housing during and after the war was difficult to find. People shared, two, three, sometimes four families to a house. We thought ourselves lucky. We only had to share with one other family, the Mudonos, a native couple and their three children. The home belonged to them. Although there was enough room, and we stayed out of each other's way, it became clear by their attitude that the Mudonos didn't like us there. No one liked having to share a home, but the war had made it a way of life."

She jerked her head up to look at me. Confusion wrinkled her brow.

"I don't know why they didn't like us. We had no choice. We weren't able to find any other place to live.

"One day Sitie Katminah suddenly doubled over with pain in her stomach. No amount of rest made the sharp, excruciating pain go away. Harry and I took her to the hospital. The doctors operated, thinking she had appendicitis. But they found nothing abnormal and closed her back up. When she recovered from surgery we took her home, but the pain continued.

"Alarmed, Harry sought the advice of his friend, Oejib. Oejib was a seamster but also a teacher of *Pentjak* [karate] and a *dukun* [healer/sorcerer]. Oejib told Harry to buy two fresh eggs at the market and that he would be over that night to see what he could do.

"When Oejib arrived, his manner frightened me. His big round eyes, usually so sweet and tender, glanced from one side of the room to the other in quick jerking movements, like the dancers of Bali looking for evil spirits. With slow, exaggerated steps he moved soundlessly across the wooden floor, from one corner to the other, looking, sniffing, waiting for I didn't know what. Then, somehow satisfied, he came toward us, his expression softening. In his customary gentle voice, he asked Sitie Katminah to lie down on the floor and expose her abdomen.

"We were all too surprised not to do as he asked. Sitie lowered herself to the floor and modestly lifted her *kabaya* [blouse] and pushed down on her sarong just enough to expose her navel.

"Oejib took one of the raw eggs Harry bought earlier. On it he wrote something. I couldn't read it. The writing was in ancient Indonesian lettering, or maybe Arabic script. He prayed while he placed the egg on Sitie's navel, then left it there for what seemed like forever. In actuality it was only a few minutes.

"The whole thing frightened me. Christians weren't supposed to do this. I became even more frightened when Oejib removed the egg. He cracked it open. Instead of a runny egg, rusty nails clattered onto the plate. Rusty nails and black powder.

"He nodded gravely and arched one of his thin eyebrows. Then he motioned for me to lie down next to Sitie.

"We went through the same procedure, and rusty nails and black powder spilled onto the plate from my egg as well. We sat on the floor, crowded around the plate, looking at each other. 'Someone is doing *goena-goena* [voodoo] on you,' Oejib said. Suddenly he snapped his head around and growled. Crawling on the floor like an animal, he sniffed the air and ground as if he'd sensed the presence of something. I didn't know what. I clung close to Harry just in case it appeared. We followed Oejib around the house, afraid to be left alone.

"In the courtyard, outside our bedroom door, Oejib came across a triangle of rough riverstones with a cluster of cut flowers in each angle. He told us to go inside—we'd be safe there. We did as we were told. Through the walls we heard him praying. We smelled incense. When he allowed us back outside, the triangle was gone, and the flowers were smoldering on a small pile beside several incense sticks.

"Oejib went on to wash away a coconut he found cracked in our entryway. He threw away pieces of a shattered watermelon on which that same strange script could be seen on the green melon skin. He burned more incense and said more prayers.

"I watched from behind Harry, not daring to say a word, but praying to my own God.

"When Oejib left, I cried. Why were people trying to hurt us? Why did I always have to live in fear?

"Harry put his arm around me and told me not to worry. He would study the ways of the dukun. No one would be able to do goena-goena to us again. But that frightened me too. 'No,' I begged him. 'Don't do such unchristian things.' But I could see Harry had already made up his mind. It wasn't my nature to challenge.

"With the help of Oejib, Harry began his training. On Friday he collected seven different kinds of flowers and bought brown and white rice. These he had to take with him to Cheribon, a holy burial place of the ancient kings. He put the rice in a white cotton bag he himself had sewn. Oejib instructed him to place the bag on the grave of one of the kings in the dark of night. He had to find the grave without the assistance of any extra light—not even a lighter or the glow of a cigarette. If he should be attacked, he could not fight back. He was to humble himself to the spirits, show respect for the site, not kill any crawling insects, frogs or snakes, not smoke, not spit, or urinate in the area.

"I begged him not to go, and when he wouldn't listen, I begged him not to go alone. In the end he took his Dutch friend, Litman, with him. Litman was an adventurous guy, and when Harry told him his plans, he thought he too might try his hand at becoming a dukun. I worried about Litman's lack of seriousness over the matter. Before they went off together, I made Harry pray the 'Our Father' with me.

"I couldn't sleep the whole time Harry was gone.

What if something happened to him? What would I do without him?

"Sitie Katminah comforted me. She had become a Christian when she met Harry's Dutch father, but she was a native and knew the ways of her people. She told me Harry's strength and determination would see him through. No harm would come to him. Still, I worried.

"When Harry returned, he came with stories that did nothing to ease my fear. The night in Cheribon had been dark and rainy. The sounds in the burial grounds were ghostly, as if a thousand eyes watched them. Without too much talk, he and Litman found two graves and placed their cotton sacks upon them. Then they backed away and waited. Litman, more nervous than he thought he'd be, had to empty his bladder behind a tree, and later, when he ignored Harry's protests and lit a cigarette, it blew up in his face."

As Aunt Dee told her story, she sat with her hands folded in her lap, her back erect. Emotion rarely showed on her face. It was as if she were recalling a dull movie. Even her voice rarely changed tone, and when it did, she sounded as if she were pleading for me to understand her.

"Harry obediently followed Oejib's instructions," Dee continued. "When it came time to gather their cotton sack and leave, Litman's sack was empty while Harry's was filled with a golden kris and an assortment of stones, blue, green, gold, purple . . .

"'The kris and the stones are for your protection,' Oejib explained to us the next day. 'Stones such as these have special powers.' This news only frightened me more. I wanted Harry to stop with this idea of becoming a dukun, but he wouldn't listen to me. He continued with his schooling.

"The trip to the graveyard had tested him. Now Harry had to fast for seven days. He existed on water and a handful of rice a day. Sitie Katminah and I told him to stop, but Harry was stubborn, a fighter. He considered himself challenged. And so he fasted. For five days he did well. Then on the sixth day, he fainted, collapsed. Sitie and I had to carry him to bed. 'You are not cut out for this belief,' I told him. 'You are too good a Christian.' Thankfully he did not pursue this crazy dukun idea anymore. I wanted him to throw the sack with the kris and magic stones away, but he convinced me that you couldn't just throw them anywhere. He'd have to find the right time and place. And so we kept them tucked away under a floorboard in our bedroom."

Aunt Dee's story of the kris and stones were similar to stories I'd heard as a child from my own mother. But my mother's stories came wrapped in humorous anecdotes as told by her native grandmother, Saitem. Saitem told of forgetful noblemen who couldn't remember where they'd left their kris, so it was a good thing the kris could fly through the air to find its master. No nobleman was considered properly dressed without his kris tucked in the back of his sash. Similarly, Saitem told stories of stones used as talismans, and if one didn't work, you looked for another.

Saitem was also Aunt Dee's grandmother, but Dee was eleven years my mother's junior and never knew Saitem. She never benefited from native stories told to children just as fairy tales are told in the United States.

"Did you have any more problems with the Mudono family or anyone else trying to do goena-goena to you?" I asked Aunt Dee.

"No, I worried about it though. And a few months later, when I became pregnant with Gina, I worried even more. All during the pregnancy I was frightened something might go wrong—more goena-goena, or what if I really did have the evil—" She stopped, rubbed her forehead, cleared her throat.

Evil what? I wanted to ask, but Aunt Dee quickly went on.

"Gina was born nine months later, beautiful, fair, with green eyes like her Dutch ancestors. A good, healthy baby at first. Then, when she was about a year and a half, she became ill with the kidney disease that would trouble her all her life. Poor little Gina. She had high fevers, blood in the urine, pain. She lost her appetite and began to waste away. I became hysterical. I had seen so much sickness, so much death . . ."

I could practically see Aunt Dee's mind racing back in time. Further and further to memories she wouldn't yet release. Held-back tears brimmed her eyes.

"The doctor put Gina on antibiotics," Aunt Dee said, her voice hollow and dry.

"Were you still living in the same house with the Mudono family?"

"Yes. Time had not made them any friendlier. But now I was wise to signs of goena-goena. I prayed daily for God to keep us safe. I swept the courtyard around our room every morning. I washed the floors in the house twice a day. No black magic dust, flowers, stones, fruit peels, nothing would I let get by me.

"I prayed for us to find a place of our own, for life to become easier. Instead it became more and more impossible. *Indos* [Dutch-Indonesian mix] like us, who did not leave when Indonesia got her independence and refused to take Indonesian citizenship, became a people without a country. The Indonesian government blacklisted us. I lost my job. So did Harry. We had no choice but to leave the country. But where could we go? Holland wouldn't take us. We had not been loyal to her. It was 1957. We didn't leave when all the other Dutch left in 1947 and '48, and we had no proof of our Dutch ancestry. The war destroyed all that.

"I cried and cried, but Harry didn't lose hope. He made arrangements for his mother to marry a senile old Dutchman. Harry arranged, through the Red Cross, for the Dutchman to get safely to Holland and be placed in a nursing home. In return, the Dutchman would allow Harry's underaged brother and sister to travel out of the country with his passport.

"The Dutchman agreed, and although Sitie Katminah hated the idea, she married him. Her two young children left for Holland where they were placed in a foster home until she could join them. She would not leave Harry, me, and baby Gina.

"Harry worked on getting copies of our papers. He wrote to the governmental authorities in the Netherlands. He talked to the Salvation Army officials. And when nothing happened, we sent a picture of Harry, Gina, and me, along with a personal letter to the prince of the Netherlands. We hoped, as head of the household, the prince would convince the queen.

"We had all but given up hope when our prayers

were answered. Major Smith, from the Salvation Army, came to our house early one morning and pulled Harry, Sitie, and me into a quiet corner and told us the Dutch Consulate in the Netherlands had given us a visa to enter Holland. We were to leave on the passenger ship, the *Waterman*. We were not to tell anyone. Our departure could be sabotaged.

"A day before we left, we gave our house key to the governor of housing, telling him we would be in East Java for a week. At three the next morning we sneaked out of the house, climbing out our bedroom window so as not to wake the Mudono family. We took only what we could carry. Furniture and other possessions, we left behind. We hurried into the waiting taxi. Even the driver didn't know our destination until we were well along on the road to Jakarta Harbor.

"The road through the *Puntjak* [mountain] curved and wound sharply. Rice paddies, banana trees, and coconut palms gave way to the higher-elevation plantations of tangerines, tea, and tobacco. The drive would take us several hours. We worried about making it to the harbor in time. God was with us. We arrived just as the ship blasted its last warning of 'all ashore who's going ashore.'

"Our journey to Rotterdam took one month. Rough seas kept us below deck, but in the Straits of Gibraltar, Harry and I ventured out. Finally we tossed the cotton sack with the kris and the magic stones overboard. I breathed easier, relieved to be rid of them. Rid of those forces."

Aunt Dee shook her head. "We did the right thing." Something happened later that convinced us even more that the stones and the kris were part of black magic.

"Unbeknownst to us, Harry's younger brother, John, had taken one of the stones and kept it. Later, when we were all in Holland, and John was in the Dutch military, several young Ambonese men ambushed him. John is a gentle, sweet man, but when those five men attacked him, he fought like a demon. Something possessed him, he told us. He had power he had never felt before. It frightened him that the yellow gold stone in his pocket could be responsible for his superhuman strength. He quickly threw it away."

"He wasn't hurt in the fight?" I asked.

"No. The other men were. Frightening isn't it? John would never hurt anyone."

I nodded. Frightening, and strange. Very strange.

Azurite

Clear and deep
as the sea,
inner guidance whispers,
travels through dark
passages
to arrive at wisdom
and revelations.

Two

AUNT DEE OPENED the door but did not wait there as I entered. The weather had become windy, unusual for late March in Southern California. She hurried away from the gusts that whipped around her front porch. We weren't experiencing our regular weather patterns. El Niño was expected to bring copious amounts of rainfall this coming winter, but even now, I could feel differences. Spring didn't meander in on crisp mornings and warming days. Instead, the wind carried a lingering chill, and billowy clouds rolled in and out.

I closed the door quickly, left my shoes at the entry, and followed Aunt Dee into the living room.

"I try to stay out of the wind," she said. "The cold and rain as well. They pierce my bones, aggravate my arthritis."

"How are you doing?" I asked, automatically assessing her. She looked remarkably well for someone who'd lost her husband so recently. Too well. I wondered if she ever broke down and cried. I hoped so.

"I'm okay," she said. "I have good moments and bad." She fumbled at her sweater button. "I had a little trouble getting dressed this morning. Without Harry everything is much slower."

She wore loose-fitting black pants, a white blouse with a neat collar, a gray sweater, and white cotton socks. Her hair, as usual, was neatly combed, and her lipstick a shade of soft red. Her swollen hands looked tender, and redder than the last time we met.

She rubbed her hands self-consciously. "They're not so bad," she said. "It's nothing like those first months when the arthritis came back. The pain was so intense I thought dying would be easier."

I knew rheumatoid arthritis was a painful disease in which the body attacked its own tissues. I also knew that, in most respects, the illness remained a mystery. Researchers agree stress is a big factor, but stress is one of those words I dislike. How do you define stress? How do you measure it?

I asked my aunt what she remembered about her life just before her relapse in 1985. Perhaps I could find a specific event, a hidden fear, a clue, anything. Something to help me help her.

She closed her eyes to think. She didn't take long.

"It all started with my bunion surgery," she said. "Hospitals have always frightened me terribly, but I had no choice. My feet hurt all the time. I couldn't walk in normal shoes." She looked down at her feet, the deformed joints bulging through the white cotton socks like stones in a cloth bag. "I still can't wear normal shoes. I never will again."

She sat quietly for a moment, looking at her feet, while her right thumb rhythmically moved over the joint of her left index finger. Back and forth, over the red, hard nodule.

I waited. Some inner strength had guided her to start this unburdening. I didn't feel I needed to push.

"And then there was the problem with Gina," she said softly, as if testing her voice. "She had divorced her husband and was living with some awful man, not from our congregation. He had gotten her pregnant. We told her she was living in sin. Even after she married him, though, Harry wouldn't speak to her. He didn't want me to speak to her either. What could we do? She disgraced our family, left our faith.

"I was torn between doing right in God's eyes and worrying about my Gina. The infection she got as a child left her with the use of only one kidney. Would she have difficulty in child birth? Would she get an infection they couldn't control? She had no money and would have to deliver at the county hospital. I worried about her. I worried about the baby. I had always wanted to be a good grandmother, to help take care of my grandchildren, give them what I never got. Harry said, 'not like this'. He wanted her to leave this crazy man she had married. He wanted her to come back to our faith, to ask the Lord God to forgive her sins."

Aunt Dee spoke as if she'd had no choice in the way things were handled. It appeared as though she'd lived in a world of black or white, wrong or right, and "right" was with her husband. Her conflicted pain, however, was obvious. Though she spoke nearly in a monotone, her eyes softened when she talked of Gina. Her body became more rigid when she mentioned Harry, and how he wouldn't give in.

I became conflicted myself. I couldn't understand why Uncle Harry had refused to help his daughter. I couldn't understand why Aunt Dee had not insisted upon helping her. Where was right and wrong? What was sin? Who does one obey? God, husband, or your own conscious?

I guessed these same thoughts tortured Aunt Dee. Would that be enough "stress" to trigger an arthritic response? I wasn't sure. Certainly Aunt Dee had been placed in a tug-of-war position. Not being her nature to challenge her husband, she had to have been left with an inner feeling of helplessness. I sensed there was more. I needed to know how she got so helpless to begin with. Why wouldn't she challenge her husband? My mind was clicking away with thoughts, but I forced my attention back on my aunt, for she was continuing with her story.

"I managed to get through the bunion surgery," Aunt Dee said, "and while I recovered I thought of Gina, day and night. But we didn't talk.

"I seemed to be recovering well when, from out of nowhere, the pain began. I felt it first in my joints, my hands, my feet. A dull ache that couldn't be relieved by aspirin. At first I didn't think too much about it. But then it came more and more often, stayed longer. Soon the pain spread throughout my body. Harry took me to the doctor, who ran several blood tests, then sent me to a specialist who diagnosed my rheumatoid arthritis.

"I was terrified of what that meant. What would happen to my life now? The doctor started me on Ascriptin. I needed it for the pain. But the pain didn't stop. The doctor increased the dose. Still the pain didn't go away. The doctor changed the medication to something stronger—naproxsen, Voltaren, Feldene. Daily I took the medication, but the pain never left. It lingered in my joints, silent for a day or so, then erupting with new force. I felt frightened, out of control, and confused.

"In the midst of all this we got a letter from Gina. She had delivered a healthy little boy. She left an address where we could reach her, but Harry would still have nothing to do with her. And I couldn't go against him. My duty was to obey my husband."

I pressed my lips together, took a deep breath. My insides were in a whirl of judgement, but I kept them to myself. I found myself wanting to understand the inner depths of her psychological makeup.

Aunt Dee rubbed her forehead between the eyebrows. She looked as if she were traveling down a long path of memories.

"I was not there for her," she said. Her soft, childlike voice was filled with sadness and guilt, emotions I hadn't heard before. Tears pooled but did not flow. "I couldn't be there." She looked down at her hands. "Gina. She had to have her baby alone. I wasn't there. I wasn't there for her." She dabbed at her eyes with a tissue and blinked the tears back. She would not allow them to flow freely. "Thank God she didn't have any complications," she said prayerfully.

She cleared her throat several times. "I couldn't be there for Gina because of my own problems."

Was she trying to convince me or herself? What problems? Her arthritis? Or was she hinting at something else? She sounded as if she wanted forgiveness but from whom? Gina? God? Certainly not me. It was not mine to give.

"It was an awful time," Aunt Dee continued. "I cried for no reason. I had night sweats, no energy, and became more and more depressed. Only Harry knew how little I slept. I woke up every morning crying. The stiffness in my bones had to be massaged out before I could be helped out of bed. Harry fixed my food. He knew what I liked, and I tried to eat what he made for me. But sometimes the pain was too much. Sometimes I thought I couldn't go on. I'm not strong."

Aunt Dee's strained smile told me something different. I sensed hidden hardships but also strength and endurance. Buried in her stories, I suspected, were feelings that had never made it past her lips. Emotions she had quietly tucked away that had, over time, festered, rooting themselves in her gnarled hands and feet.

"Harry kept me alive with his encouragement, support, and love," she said. "If it wasn't for Harry I don't know what would have become of me. I owe him my life you know. He saved me." Her smile faded, and her eyes took on a distant look.

The war had been over for some time, she explained. She was living with her Aunt Erika and Uncle William. They had three daughters and a son, all older. She lived at the back of their house in a small storage room.

"I liked it," she said. "It allowed me to study undisturbed late into the night." Her days were filled with school and the many chores Aunt Erika conjured for her. In exchange for room and board, she swept the floors, watched her aunt's grandchild, did the grocery shopping at dawn, and a host of other little things. "But I fretted," she said. "I wanted to do something I could be proud of.

"Somehow I managed to get through school and receive a diploma in secretarial skills. Aunt Erika discouraged me from looking for a job. She didn't think it necessary, nor that I was capable. She believed I . . ." Aunt Dee stopped. She swallowed several times. A single tear rolled down her smooth face. "Evil eye. She believed I had the evil eye upon me." She wiped the tear away with the tip of her index finger. "But one of my chores was to mop the tile floors of the dining room. And in the corner on a pedestal stood the large family Bible. I wasn't allowed to touch it, but I did. I opened it each time to a different Psalm, and while I walked back and forth with the mop, I would carefully, making sure not to be seen, glance at the words. 'Yahweh is my shepherd, I lack nothing. In meadows of green grass he lets me lie. To the waters of repose he leads me; there he revives my soul. . . .' [Psalm 23] I took comfort in the Bible. It gave me strength. I believe the Bible guided me, gave me the determination to go out and find a job.

"One morning, instead of doing Aunt Erika's grocery shopping, I stopped at Jacobson van den Berg Export and Import. Before I could lose my nerve, I marched up to the personnel department and got an interview with Mr. Townsend. He tested me on my stenographic dictation, typing, and bookkeeping. To my surprise, he was pleased and asked if I could start the following morning. Stunned and delighted, I told him 'yes,' but I was left with the fear of how I would tell Aunt Erika."

A little glimmer of light danced in Aunt Dee's eyes. She liked that she'd been strong and had done what she felt she needed to. My guess was that it didn't happen often.

"All that day I said nothing," Dee continued with her story. "I couldn't sleep that night because I still hadn't said anything and I had to be at work by 9:00 a.m. When morning finally came, I had made up my mind. Nothing could stop me from taking that job. I had to do it or I wouldn't survive. I had to. And so I dressed in the only other good dress I had, fixed my hair, and went into the main house to make my aunt's coffee and breakfast, as she always expected me to.

"She noticed my dress immediately and asked why I was dressed like that. She looked me up and down like a cat hungrily eyeing a gecko on the wall. I placed her cup of coffee in front of her. As casually as I could, I told her I had a job.

"Her puffy round face reddened. She stared at me. I backed up a few steps.

"I told her I could pay for my board now, but she didn't respond. I could feel her anger, her disapproval. It frightened me. I lived in fear of doing something wrong, of displeasing her, others, God. But it was a good job, an honest job, a decent-paying job, and so before she could stop me, I said good-bye and left. And although she didn't need the little money I made, at the end of the month she took most of it."

"What about Uncle William?" I interrupted. "Didn't he have anything to say?"

Aunt Dee moved her head slowly from side to side. "Uncle William was a dear, sweet man, but I think he was afraid of Aunt Erika too. They seldom interacted with one another. Aunt Erika controlled everything. He didn't say much. He slept in the storage room next to mine. I don't know why he didn't sleep in the house. I guessed he liked being away from her. I never asked."

A little smile pulled at Dee's lips.

"He was hard of hearing. It was difficult to communicate with him. But often at night, when I studied by oil lamp, he'd knock on my door, come in, and see if I was alright. I felt sorry for him. He felt out of place. So did I. When I told him I had gotten a job, his eyes sparkled and he broke out into a bright smile.

"His smile, and knowing I had risked my aunt's wrath by standing firm, made me proud of myself. Work was a new beginning for me."

"That's where you met Harry?"

Dee nodded. "I met him the first day on the job. Introducing myself to the other workers, I suddenly saw somebody I recognized. Harry. He had been my sports trainer when I was in high school. Of course with my ugly braids gone, he didn't recognize me. We had a good laugh over it when I told him.

"Six months later when he dictated a letter to me, he had me sign it with '1000 kisses.' I blushed, realizing the kisses were for me. I couldn't remember the last time anyone showed me that kind of affection. I wanted to cry, but that would have been stupid. I panicked when he asked if he could meet my family. If he met my aunt, everything would be ruined. He took my hand pretending to read my palm, but instead looked deep into my eyes. I don't know why, but at that moment I knew I could trust him. I needed to trust him. I needed to tell someone about the horrible things that had happened to me. So as we ate lunch, I told him everything."

Aunt Dee looked at me, then back at her hands. With her thumb she made small circular motions over one swollen finger joint, then another.

"Well, almost everything." She paused, looked up at me. "Harry was so sweet. He listened, shared some of his own horrors, his illegitimate birth because his father could not marry his mother—he was still tied to his first wife, who was crazy and locked in an asylum. He hinted at problems with his older stepsister and brother, who had difficulty accepting him because he was the product of their father's native concubine. He told me of the war years, the camp years, the years he studied like a madman so he could make something of himself.

"And when he took my hand and held it in his, he made me feel safe. It felt warm and nice, a feeling I'd forgotten."

She paused a moment, as if remembering his touch on hers again. Then with a sigh she continued.

"Aunt Erika didn't like Harry. That I should have someone interested in me angered her. One evening while Harry visited me, she came out of her room, stood right in front of us, her face red and her eyes big and wild. In a loud voice, she asked Harry if he was blind. 'Do you really want to marry a girl whose family is all dead? A girl who suffers from who knows what?'

"A pain shot through my chest as if she had driven a burning knife into my heart. I could find no words in self-defense. I just sat there, fists clenched tight, weeping inwardly.

"Then I felt Harry's hand on mine. His touch gave me strength. He told Aunt Erika he already knew my past, loved me, and still wanted to marry me. For a moment they glared at each other, then Harry gave my hand a squeeze and excused himself for the evening.

"We dated for a year, and at the end of that year he asked Aunt Erika if she would give her permission for us to marry.

"She answered with a cool 'no.' She gave no explanation. I was only nineteen. She knew I needed to be twenty-one before the authorities would allow us to marry without permission. To make matters worse, Aunt Erika ordered me out of her house. I panicked. It was the only home I knew." Dee shook her head. "She made no sense. I couldn't get married, but she could throw me out into the streets. I wished I had been strong enough to pack my bags and go, but I wasn't. I was frightened, and she knew it. She took pleasure in my fear. Thankfully, Uncle William came to my rescue. He wouldn't hear of me being turned out into the street. Though he had very little power over my aunt and could not get her to give marital consent, he managed to convince her that throwing me out of the house would not be acceptable.

"I stayed in my little storage-room bedroom, communicating only with my uncle. My aunt grew more stubborn with the weeks and months. She still expected my monthly salary, but never said a word to me, and guarded her pantry so I couldn't eat anything. Sometimes, if my aunt wasn't in the kitchen, the servants slipped me a little of their food—rice with leftover shrimp heads, chicken feet, and vegetables.

"One day, when I could no longer keep quiet, I told Harry. He flew into a rage. He wrote Aunt Erika a letter asking her to explain this situation, and he drafted copies for all the relatives. He was like that, a "take control" type of person. People didn't get away with things around Harry."

Uncle Harry had been head of his family since his father died. Forced into early manhood, he looked after his mother and his younger brother and sister. When Harry's mother heard about Dee's mistreatment, she took it upon herself to make sure that Dee got food. She sent Harry's little brother, John, to Dee's work every day with a lunch basket. In the evening, Harry picked her up on his motorcycle and took her to his home for dinner.

"With Sitie Katminah, Harry, John, and his sister, Christien, I finally felt like I had a real family, people who cared about me. We were married as soon as I turned twenty-one." Aunt Dee looked at me with the first genuine smile I had seen on her face. A softness touched her tight forehead. "You see," she said. "Harry really is—was—my hero." She took a deep breath, looked down at her hands, and with one finger traced the length of another finger. She looked up at me. "Sometimes I'm angry he left me."

She shifted her glance to look around the room. She didn't like to say anything negative about anyone. She always apologized when something inadvertently slipped out. She denied herself anger when she told her stories of Aunt Erika. She told the stories as if Aunt Erika could not be blamed for her behavior. She didn't even like to say she was angry with Harry for dying. Might God hear her and think less of her?

Was this a pattern? When did it start? I needed to know more. The pages of written material Dee had originally handed to me were like skeletons of moments in time. There was no flesh to them. No feelings expressed. A superficial time line. I felt like an archeologist dusting the surface of a treasure chest.

"Are you okay here by yourself?" I asked, now knowing how Uncle Harry had helped her bathe, gotten her dressed in the morning, and prepared her food.

"I'm fine. Jeff and his wife call often. They live in San Clemente but are planning to move closer, and Gina lives only five minutes away. I can drive. Not far, but I can get to the market, to Gina's, to see friends of mine. At night the only place I go is to Bible meetings. Friends pick me up. I'm afraid to drive by myself at night."

"Your relationship with Gina is good then."

"Oh yes. It wasn't easy at first. Rex, her son, was a big help. He's twelve now. Very bright. He's in the gifted program. He comes over after school. During the summer he comes and swims. I don't need to do much for him. In fact, he does more for me."

She boasted like any true grandmother.

"Harry finally gave in. I was in so much pain the year Rex was born that Harry looked for ways to distract me. He contacted Gina, and she came right away with the baby. We loved seeing little Rex, but Gina tried our patience. She wore clothes unbecoming a young lady, way too tight and mostly black. Her hair was always tinted a different color. Sometimes bright green, then red, even purple." Aunt Dee grinned uncomfortably. "Gina was so wild then. She looked unnatural. She was still with that man we disapproved of, and we didn't like the company they kept either. Wild party people, with strange haircuts and rings through their noses. Gina came so we could enjoy the baby, but she kept us at a distance.

"The pain medication I needed kept me bedridden most of the time. Watching Rex, holding him, was a happy distraction. But I could hear Gina with her father in the other room. She was never one to back down from him. It hurt me to hear them argue. Then, she'd go home frustrated, and Harry would be angry for the rest of the day and well into the evening.

"I suffered for months, pain waking me daily, and the feeling of fear pressing down on me. I took medication after medication. Then my weight began to plummet. By the end of the first year, I weighed eighty-five pounds. I looked anorexic. Friends raised a curious eye. I became weaker and weaker and thought for sure I was dying. But a colonoscopy revealed internal bleeding. The doctor took me off Voltaren. The bleeding stopped. I began to gain weight again. The doctor then started me on a regimen of Plaquenil, an antimalaria drug, but that did little to relieve my discomfort.

"Again, Harry saved me. He gave me the courage to try treatments other than what my doctor recommended. Harry encouraged me to see a chiropractor who specialized in chronic illness. For six months I saw him once a week. His gentle manipulations and the working of acupressure points did some good. He was expensive, though, and my insurance did not cover his therapy. So I stopped.

"For a while I tried a woman who combined massage therapy with submerging my hands in water and giving me low voltage shocks. Her treatments did nothing for me. They only served to make me feel helpless about my condition. But Harry wouldn't let me give up.

"Harry," she repeated softly. She looked over at me with a half-smile. "We were supposed to go to Holland and visit his family this summer. We were both looking forward to it."

"You can still go," I said.

"By myself?" Her voice sounded startled, though her eyes kept their pensive look. "No. I could never do that. I've never been anywhere without Harry. I've never been anywhere alone."

"Go with someone else. A friend, one of your children."

She shook her head. "They can't leave their work. It's okay. Perhaps the family will visit me here."

Then she was quiet. I wanted to fill the space her silence made, but I let it be. During my years as a nurse, I've learned that silence can be good. But it requires patience.

I waited.

"You know it's strange," Aunt Dee said, after a while. "After Harry died I had a dream. I can still remember it clearly." She gave an nervous little laugh.

"I know dreams are crazy," she said. "You dream only if you're upset. They don't mean anything. Except for the dreams in the Bible," she quickly added. "Those are different."

How are they different? I wanted to know but didn't ask. Instead I asked her to tell me about her dream.

She leaned back into the couch. "It happened a day or two after Harry died. I was standing by myself in a desert, waiting for Harry. The sand behind me and all around was loose. In the distance, I saw a red VW Bug coming toward me. It's Harry in the car. He's driving over the loose sand as if it were nothing. 'Hold on!' he shouts. He means, to the bumper of the VW. I grab hold, expecting him to let me into the car, but he doesn't. I hold on as hard as I can because I know if I let go I will die. I hold on all the way through the loose sand and until we get onto a road. I expect him to stop, but he doesn't. So I let go. Harry drives off."

She looked at me and slowly shrugged her shoulders.

"That's it. I told you. It's silly."

I felt like I'd been hit with a stone between the eyes. Silly? It seemed to me, Aunt Dee had been given a choice. In the dream, Harry had left her on a road in the desert. In the desert! Did that mean she could now choose to make this earth her wasteland, dwell in helplessness—or find solace and spiritual growth? Her psyche seemed to be telling her that Harry had taken her as far as he could. She could manage her own life now. She was not helpless.

I had to get her to talk more about the things that frightened and hurt her. I began to suspect that her illness resulted from an accumulation of life circumstances that had beaten her down. To examine 1984, the year prior to the onset of her arthritis, as many of the medical journals suggested, was not enough. I felt that the immediate stress of her hospitalization for bunion surgery, and the strained relationship between herself, Harry, and Gina were factors—but could there be something deeper? Something so awful that it finally forced her into a self-imposed stone prison?

Ojo Caliente

Ojo Caliente,
the Timekeepers, remind
that underground tributaries feed
springs, energize and enliven nature
just as music
from our past
plays over our soul
then rests
in the cliffs of our body.

Three

EAGERLY, I MET my aunt again.

It was late April. Spring had been kept at bay, and the afternoons were still cool. We decided to make something warm to drink before we settled into our talk. Aunt Dee had placed a few danishes on dainty flowered china, which I carried out to the living room coffee table. Piano music played softly from the stereo—Chopin, I think. The sound was soothing, and the room had a lightness I hadn't noticed before. I looked around, trying to detect the source. Open shades? An overhead fixture? Nothing so concrete. The lightness was more of an essence, like the fragrance of a flower—present, but not visible.

I returned to the kitchen, where Aunt Dee was pouring the hot water for tea. It surprised me how well she managed with the limited mobility of her fingers. I complimented her.

"They've been like this for nearly ten years," she said. "I've grown used to them." She added a heaping teaspoon of honey to her cup and offered me some. I shook my head no. She stirred her tea slowly, then rinsed the spoon off and placed it on a paper towel to dry.

"I believe," she said, "my fingers and toes became like this because of the gold injections my rheumatologist suggested."

I rummaged through my memory. "I didn't know deformities were a side effect."

"Nor do doctors," Dee said. "I believe differently."

I carried both teacups to the living room, the aroma of cinnamon and cloves rising in the steam. Aunt Dee settled herself on the couch, and I sat in the love seat, turned towards her at an angle.

"Before I started the injections my hands and feet were not deformed," Aunt Dee said. She shook her head. "My rheumatologist told me I would have to take a full treatment. Three months. I was so miserable, I blindly took anyone's advice. I started the shots. They were very painful. They left me weak, nauseated, and with pain radiating down my legs. I endured the shots, but the promised relief didn't come. In fact, the pain intensified. Then one morning I noticed my fingers. The big joints didn't look

the same. A redness just below the surface was barely noticeable, but I could feel a difference in my
joints. A hardness.

"I made an appointment with my rheumatologist
and showed him my hands. I told him I believed the
injections were to blame, but he assured me that was
not the case. He told me my hands were fine, a little
swelling of the joints was to be expected with my illness. Still, I refused to take any more injections. The
doctor told me to go talk to another rheumatologist.

"I did. But the damage had been done. Almost
overnight my joints grew worse. My fingers and
toes swelled. I couldn't walk. I could barely eat by
myself."

Her spark of rebelliousness toward the injections
indicated to me that an intuitive part of her still flick-
ered somewhere deep within. I couldn't help but
feel once again that locked in her past were the keys
to her future.

We sipped our tea, looking at each other over the
rims of the china cups, momentarily lost in our own
thoughts.

"How did you come to live at Aunt Erika's?" I
asked between sips. From Aunt Dee's handwritten
pages, I had a vague notion of what she might
answer, but she'd left out so many details. I needed
clarification. I wanted her to tap into those underground tributaries where her emotions flowed.
Where her secrets lay.

Aunt Dee swallowed as she placed her cup on
the table. "My sister, brother, and I were war
orphans," she explained. "The Dutch law was very
clear. We had no choice. We had to live with our
closest male relative. Actually, we should have
come to your grandfather, the older of the Van Gils

brothers, but he too had died as a prisoner of war, and so we were ordered to go to Uncle William, a younger brother. I was only ten at the time. My brother, Boetje, was thirteen, and my sister, Nita, almost fifteen.

"Uncle William and his oldest daughter, Helen, came to pick us up from the Red Cross government housing. We must have been a sight: clean, but scabbed from bites and boils, deathly thin, and wearing all but rags. The three of us were frightened. Our life had been one of not knowing who to trust. We clung to one another and spoke very little. Helen was kind. She asked if we wouldn't like to come live with her and her family.

"I was sad to leave Anna Yacobs behind. She was a friend of my father's and had taken care of us through some awful years."

An involuntary shudder rippled over Aunt Dee. She blinked back tears as if forcing one memory down in order to stay with the one at hand.

"Anna wanted to keep me, but the three of us could not be separated, and we did not want to be. We did as we were told and went home with Uncle William and Helen. But once 'home,' even at my young age, I could feel my Aunt Erika wasn't pleased to have us. She didn't greet us with open arms, kiss our sunken cheeks, or ask if we wanted or needed anything. We were children who had survived against many odds. We needed kindness. We needed understanding. But we got none of these. We settled on having a place to stay and were content with that.

"War destroys so much. For me, for us three, life had been shattered. We no longer had a mother who loved us, told us stories, and kissed away our hurts. We no longer had a father, whose lap we could crawl into for safety, who created special games for us, and played the violin so beautifully.

"There was no harmony and tranquillity at Aunt Erika's home, only discord. Uncle William, nearly deaf, kept to himself. Helen spent most of her time with her fiancé, whom Aunt Erika disliked. Piet, their son, lived in another town, and Enny, another daughter, followed her Japanese husband back to Japan. I was too young to concern myself then, but oh how Aunt Erika must have been upset about one of her daughters running off with a Japanese—one of the enemy.

"Only Nora, the youngest daughter, really lived there," Dee continued. "And she lived as a princess, getting everything her way, paying little attention to us. Why should she? We were so much younger. Perhaps it was a burden to have to take on three more children when you've already raised four of your own. And times were not easy. But we were family, and not bad children. We didn't deserve to be treated as if we had the 'evil eye.' It wasn't our fault we were orphaned.

"My sister, brother, and I were given the garage to live in. We didn't mind. We had comfortable beds, lights, and drawers for clothes we might some-day have. It smelled a little of mold, but that too, we didn't mind. We had experienced far worse. We ate good food. The rice was clean and white, the vegeta-bles weren't rotten, and the curried chicken felt warm and nice on my stomach. I could only eat small amounts though. More than a little made me throw up. Nita told me we used to eat like this all the time, but for me those days were misty dreams.

"We started back to school, and on afternoons when we finished with our school work, Helen and her fiancé rewarded us by letting us take a walk around the neighborhood with them. I liked this. It reminded me of the days when we had a mother and father. A time when I could walk unafraid. When I didn't have to look over my shoulder, wondering where danger might come from.

"School was difficult for all of us. Me, because it had been such a long time, and I didn't remember much. Helen had to teach me how to read and write all over again. Boetje's health burdened him. He never fully recovered from the malaria, and the wound on his leg would not heal. Occasionally it still oozed green pus. He often became weak. He tried not to let it show, but I knew. He became more quiet. Didn't move around much. Spent more time studying. He was an excellent student and helped others with their homework, especially math. Some students gave him thank-you presents. He liked being cared about. He looked for ways to make people like him.

"He cooked *nasih goreng* [fried rice with butter, egg, and hot peppers] because he knew Aunt Erika liked it. He drew beautiful pictures of flowers and trees for Nora, and he planted *kadja-piring* [gardenias] in front of the garage to make it look nice. He said it was for the family, but I knew it was especially for me. I always loved flowers.

"Boetje was a gentle and affectionate brother, the only one who would cuddle and kiss me. But Aunt Erika didn't allow such behavior. She told us it was indecent and threatened to send him to the orphanage if she caught us.

"Nita was the quietest. There were so many things I wanted to talk to her about, to ask my older sister, because I figured she would know. But she refused to talk. She told me not to think about the past. 'Never think about what happened. Just forget it.' I knew she had painful memories too, and sometimes we'd just sit together and cry.

"Our life was not bad while we had each other. We drew comfort in being together, knowing that someone loved us, feeling a connection to the time when all seemed right with the world. But we never spoke of our feelings: our fears, our anger, our confusion. Those, we kept to ourselves. And when they came forward in nightmares, we pressed them back down, focused our minds elsewhere.

"So even when Boetje went in and out of the hospital, I didn't question. I knew he was sick—his leg, the malaria. I also knew the nurses loved him. They called him the gentle gray-eyed boy, and I believed they would take good care of him. I believed . . . I believed," she repeated, caught in her own memory. Her voice softened to a raspy whisper. Her eyes turned liquid. Then, perhaps realizing she had drifted too deep into forgotten pain, she apologized and continued from the place she had left off. Her voice, for a moment sad and revealing, changed quickly back to its controlled distance.

"One day Boetje became so sick, he had to have several blood transfusions. Nita and I visited him in the hospital, tried to cheer him up, and though he laughed he never became well enough to come home. We visited him daily and lit candles for him in church. We prayed and prayed.

"But he died." Aunt Dee took a deep breath. Her lower lip quivered and she bit down to stop it. "Nita and I felt so guilty." Her already liquid eyes filled with more tears. "We weren't there for him," she said slowly, swallowing great lumps of sorrow, a lone tear escaping the corner of her eye.

I could feel her hanging on, not wanting to lose control, not wanting to see the images that were forcing their way into her memory.

"It's okay to cry," I said.

She reached for a napkin from the table and dabbed at her eyes. She took her time, composed herself.

"We weren't with him when he took his last breath," she said.

I moved beside her and placed an arm around her shoulders. "It's okay," I whispered, hoping she would cry, that she would release her pain. But she wouldn't. It was almost as if she couldn't cry.

"I was angry," she continued in her controlled, distant voice. "We were supposed to be together, always. I wanted to know why this had to happen. But there was no one who could answer me. Helen might have been able to help, but by then she had married and no longer lived at home. My sister couldn't give me any answers either. Nita became pale and sick for a long while after Boetje died. She never fully recovered. Not only was she more quiet than ever, but she spent less time at home. She busied herself with school and friends, and we didn't even have those moments when we cried together.

"When Nita graduated from high school, Aunt Erika expected her to do more work around the house. To make extra money, Aunt Erika now rented out rooms. Some of the renters were business and military men. Others were sick people looking for a better climate in our small mountain town. I kept my distance from them. They smoked too much and coughed all the time, spitting everywhere, sometimes spitting blood. Aunt Erika assigned Nita the job of cleaning up after these people.

"I noticed one of the renters always watched Nita. I didn't like the way he looked at her, the way he tried to touch her while she worked. I was only fifteen, but I knew danger. I warned Nita. She tried to stay away from him.

"One day I found Nita in tears. She was packing her few belongings. Aunt Erika had thrown her out of the house. Gossiping guests told Aunt Erika they saw Nita go into the bathhouse with one of the guests—that man. Nita never had a chance to explain her side. She packed quickly and left without telling me where she would be.

"For months I didn't hear from Nita, and no one in the family cared that I was miserable. I cried and cried because she was all I had left in the world. But all my tears did nothing.

"I looked for her whenever I walked through the streets, but I never saw her.

"Finally, a note arrived telling me Nita was very sick and in the hospital. A married couple, friends of hers, had been taking care of her. I went to see her right away. She was in a large room with curtains drawn around several other beds. When I stepped inside the curtain to Nita's bed, I wept at the sight of her. I'd never seen her so pale and gray. Even her dark eyes seemed drained of color, and she didn't attempt a smile when she saw me. She explained she had been dragged into the bathroom by Aunt Erika's renter. Raped. Gotten pregnant. Miscarried. And now she had an infection.

"I wiped a thin strand of mousy brown hair from her face and kissed her moist cheeks. She only looked at me, almost through me. In barely a whisper she told me not to cry.

"I visited her every day, trying to cheer her up, trying to give her strength, but she grew steadily weaker. No one else in the family knew Nita was in the hospital. She wanted it that way. I was her only family, she told me.

"I prayed hard for her health to return, but she continued to weaken. I became frightened and felt I should tell someone. I couldn't stand carrying this burden by myself. I told Aunt Erika. Instead of compassion and understanding, she laughed. She laughed hatefully, told me it was the mark of the 'evil eye' on my sister and me. We were a cursed family, she told me.

"She did nothing for my Nita. No one did. I continued visiting Nita on my own, carrying my sorrow with me and telling only God.

"Within weeks Nita had shrunken away to a skeleton. She had lost the will to live. She handed me her gold cross necklace. 'Don't wear it,' she told me, dropping it into my hand. 'Don't wear it.'

"I didn't know what she meant. God had always been a part of my life. A part of her life too. We had been baptized at birth, gone to bed with Bible stories, trusted in God's knowing. But she was giving up. Nita wasn't trying to survive.

"My eyes were so full of tears that day, I could hardly see the way home. My heart ached. My body felt stiff, as if I couldn't move. I knew Nita was dying, and I had no one to turn to. I prayed that God would relieve her suffering. At that moment I found myself in front of a church. Hymns, as if sung by angels, floated out to me. I followed the music inside. There I spoke to the pastor, told him about Nita, and asked him, begged him, to visit her. He promised he would.

"The next day, the police came to notify the family of Nita's death. Alone, I bore my sorrow. Like with my brother, I wasn't there for her when she took her last breath. I felt guilty. I felt angry. I felt abandoned. I longed to talk to someone, but there was no one. No one cared how I felt. Now, I was truly alone."

A few large tears ran across Aunt Dee's cheekbones, streaked her face. But she did not allow such an indulgence for long. She dabbed at her face, sniffed, and gathered herself as she had, no doubt, done time and time again.

She smiled timidly. The strains of Chopin had long since ended, but I thought I still heard them, soft and gentle, like loving hands caressing the soul.

River Rock

Like the river rock,
life tumbles us
downstream,
sometimes we lose
our rough edges
become smooth and easy
to step upon,
but within,
the energy
still
beats strong.

Four

I COULD NOT begin to imagine how alone Aunt Dee must have felt. Fourteen when her brother died, and then, a little over a year later, she was faced with her sister's death. She was a fifteen-year-old alone in the world. I wondered how life was for her during that time, after Nita died, before she met Harry.

Aunt Dee continued her storytelling without much prodding. As she talked, I watched for signs that I might be pushing her too much. But she appeared increasingly more comfortable, even eager, to tell me more.

"I felt empty after Nita died. No one to love. No one to love me. Aunt Erika didn't think I should have the large garage for myself. This had been my bed-room with Nita and Boetje for five years, but now Aunt Erika could use it for more renters. She decided I should sleep with her in her room. 'It would be more cosy,' she told me.

"But it was only for Aunt Erika's convenience. Every night before going to bed, Aunt Erika drank several glasses of gin or vodka. I ignored her. I had studying to do. But if she finished the bottle and needed more, she'd make me stop what I was doing and go out for another bottle. Even if I'd finished my schoolwork and had gone to sleep exhausted from the day, she'd wake me up. Make me get dressed and go out. It was always after 10:00 p.m. Everyone in the house would be asleep. She wanted me to sneak out, and make sure to hide the new bottle under a towel when I returned.

"I hated going out at that hour. It frightened me. The country wasn't safe at night. Indonesian rebels stalked the streets, made trouble, shot randomly. People let their watchdogs roam the streets after dark. Those half-wild animals would chase after me on the bicycle, and I would have to peddle fast then, pull my legs up on the handlebars to avoid their sharp jaws.

"Aunt Erika had a dog too. I didn't like him. He played in the mud and smelled. When I asked Aunt Erika if I could please have another room, so I wouldn't disturb her sleep in the morning and late at night when I studied, she put me in the room next to the kitchen with the dog. During the day, the filthy animal slept on my bed, tracking in all his mud and smelliness. If I wanted to rest in the afternoon, I'd have to rest sitting up, cowering in the corner of my bed. I was afraid he would attack me. He never did. Thankfully, the dog prowled the streets at night.

"Uncle William knew I was afraid of the dog. Everyone really knew. But I think it was Uncle William's doing that finally got me exiled to the storage room next to his. He worked in quiet ways.

"From our little rooms, Uncle William and I had little contact with Aunt Erika. He came and went, did whatever he did to keep himself busy. And I did what I had to do, which was plenty."

"It's amazing he stayed with her," I said.

Aunt Dee shrugged her shoulders. "He was a good Catholic. He read a lot and kept to himself. I did the same. School was my salvation. I studied very hard." She sighed. "It wasn't easy. Getting my studying done, I mean. There was always something Aunt Erika wanted me to do. Then Nora got married and had a baby. I became her built-in nanny. I had to do everything for the baby: watch her, feed her, put her to bed, plus do my regular cleaning and shopping chores—and still be at school by 7:00 a.m.

"Before class, I was expected to go to the *pasar baroe* [the large market]. I had to leave the house no later than 5:00 a.m. Any one of the other servants could have done the shopping, but Aunt Erika said she only trusted me to do it. I took that as a great honor." By her clear voice, and a slight lift of the chin, I knew she was genuinely proud of this status.

"I didn't have a bicycle of my own. Aunt Erika allowed me to take Nora's old bike to the market. The bike was a miserable old thing, with tires that were not filled and repaired evenly. When riding it, I must have looked like a jumping frog. Clump, clump, clumpedy-bump, plop." She laughed to herself.

I tried to picture her: a thin girl of fifteen, dark pigtails bouncing at her shoulders as she peddled in the predawn.

"I didn't mind," Dee said. "It made the trip quicker. I didn't have much time. I had to get back with the groceries and still leave myself enough time to walk the three kilometers to school. The old bike was off-limits to me for anything but the groceries.

"Going to market was a dirty business, always crowded and muddy. And Aunt Erika ordered so much food. Vegetables, potatoes, chickens, frogs. The bike made it easier to carry the heavy, smelly load, but no less messy. Blood would ooze from the slaughtered chickens and drip onto my feet. I learned not to wear my shoes, allowing the putrid liquid to drip and harden between my toes. Before setting off for school, I'd wash the caked mud and blood from my feet and slip into the only pair of shoes I owned."

She shook her head. "I'm still sensitive to smells. I like things fresh and clean. Even now when I cook at home, I open the windows so the heavy cooking smell doesn't linger indoors."

I took a deep breath, aware that the house truly had no odor—no must, no spice, no fresh-baked bread, only a subtle essence of rose from the bouquet on the coffee table.

"I didn't mind the shopping," Aunt Dee said. "Except when Aunt Erika would change her mind about some item and send me back to return it. I sometimes think she did it only to aggravate me. I never said anything. I had learned to do as I was told."

We both took a deep breath, and simultaneously reached for a danish. We laughed at the sameness of our motions, both needing a release from the gravity of her story. Aunt Dee nibbled a tiny piece of pastry. Her face was calm and sweet, without wrinkles or any trace of the pain, anger, and abandonment she'd experienced. It was as if her soul defied the illness that housed all the feelings from a past, too horrible to talk about, until now.

We kept eating, each in our own thoughts. She amazed me. Time and circumstances had beat her down, driven her inward, silenced her, and made her body stiff, but I knew that within her, the ember of life still burned. How would I fan that into a flame?

"You know," Aunt Dee said, wiping the corners of her mouth with her napkin. "I've become more careful of what is done to my body. The rheumatologist I went to after the gold injection incident wanted to immediately start me on methotrexate. It's an anti-cancer drug they say helps arthritis. I was instantly suspicious. I read up on it. It's highly toxic to the body. But my pain wasn't getting any better. Harry suggested I talk to my longtime medical doctor. I've always trusted his opinion. He eased some of my worry, advised me to take no more than three tablets of methotrexate a week. He also recommended I take the drug on the same days every week, and always at the exact same time. And, no alcohol.

"I followed his instructions. And in three weeks, I was the most free of pain that I had been since the whole thing started."

Chlorite

Just as the soft green of chlorite
bonds with the strength of quartz
to form a beautiful crystal,
ever flowing
light and energy,
so too the body
heals
with multifacets
of radiant willing and
luminous courage.

Five

THE NEXT TIME I met with Aunt Dee, we were joined by her daughter, Gina, a beautiful young woman with an olive complexion, striking green eyes, and hair streaked the color of Burgundy wine. I remembered her from family affairs we'd been to as kids. She'd always seemed drawn to slightly offbeat clothes and hairstyles.

We hugged, heart-to-heart, a custom so often done frivolously, but here I could feel the realness, instant connection.

"I wanted to come," Gina said. Her voice was strong and clear. "I hope you don't mind."

"Not at all." I was happy she'd come. Aunt Dee had mentioned that she took homeopathic medicines prescribed by her daughter, and I had questions.

Gina was genuinely pleased that her mother had found someone she could trust her stories to. She told me her mother never talked about the past. Indonesia remained a country filled with mystery but no voice. Gina was forty-one and in a place in her life where she wanted to know more about her own roots. It made her sad that her mother could not talk about such things.

As we walked into the living room, I noticed a new painting sitting on an easel in a shaft of light near the sliding glass doors. In gray tones, it depicted a young child standing on a porch, looking out to sea. The child, viewed from the back, stood in silhouette and could be either girl or boy. There was a sense of waiting, or perhaps awe, as he or she looked up into the sky. Palm trees to one side lent a tropical effect. And again, as in her earlier seascape, I felt the qualities of movement and loneliness; however, this time her sky was ablaze with yellow and orange. Aiming for a sunset, she'd managed to create a feeling of locked doors being opened.

I raised an eyebrow at my aunt.

"It's not quite finished yet," she said. "I was trying to capture a night in Hawaii." She paused, studying the painting. "Harry and I went there once. He loved it. He wanted to move there, away from all

the complaining people at work. He wanted an easier life, but I pleaded with him. We wouldn't know
anyone. Our children were grown, with lives of
their own, and wouldn't be with us." She plucked a
piece of lint from her sweater. "Sometimes I think
he didn't want to be bothered with children. It
made him mad when I would consider them before
him."

She seated herself in her usual place on the
couch. Gina sat next to her, and I took my usual spot
on the love seat. The three of us looked at each
other, smiling awkwardly, not sure how to proceed.

"Your mother tells me you do homeopathy," I said
to Gina. "Last time I heard, you were a hairdresser."

She laughed; her smile was wide and genuine, her
teeth, white and even.

"I still do a few haircuts here and there. I started
homeopathy, really, to help myself. When my son's
father and I divorced, I found myself a single
parent, and suddenly realized I needed to grow up. I
had a child to care for. I needed to take responsibil-
ity for my health. I knew I had a bad kidney, and yet I
had poured all kinds of toxins into my body."

Her green eyes looked directly into mine.

"When I was seventeen," she said, "I had a
strange dream. Maybe a nightmare would be a more
appropriate description. Over and over again I
dreamt that when I was thirty-five, I would die. I
came to believe it would really happen, but on midnight of my thirty-fifth birthday, I was still alive. My
friends called to check on me and laughed at my
ridiculousness, but something did die that night. The
old me. The rebellious me.

"In a sense I was reborn. A new energy and
curiosity enveloped me, and I couldn't let it go.
Thoughts came to me of my grandmother, Sitie

Katminah, and the herbs she brewed to make me feel better as a child. I took it as a message that I should do something with herbs. I began to study. One study led to another, and finally to Ayurveda and homeopathy. As I cleaned up my diet and lifestyle, my health improved. And as my body rid itself of the alcohol used to dull the emotional stress of my family, and the toxins I had taken for kidney pain and infection, my life changed.

"I met my present husband, whose zeal for life matches mine, and with his encouragement I furthered my study of homeopathy. He afforded me the opportunity to travel to India and work at a clinic in Calcutta. Not that he could have done anything to stop me," she quickly added, with a gleam in her eye. "I would have gone no matter what, but with his encouragement, I felt that much more at ease and comfortable about leaving my son in his care."

The green of her eyes seemed to deepen and her energy was tangible. It fascinated me that a woman as frightened of life as my aunt could have a daughter so highly charged, so open and curious.

"I helped take care of Rex, my grandson, while Gina traveled to India," Aunt Dee said in her little-girl voice.

Gina smiled as she touched her mother lightly on the leg. "Homeopathy brought us closer together. Huh?"

Aunt Dee answered with a shy smile.

As I looked at mother and daughter together, I felt my aunt's meekness, saw a dull, resigned-to-life's-suffering kind of helplessness. Gina, on the other hand, radiated strength.

"How so?" I asked. "How did homeopathy bring you closer?"

"You know, when you're sick like this," Aunt Dee

said, "you reach a point where you just can't do anything about it. You begin looking for reasons why
you have the sickness. I wanted to find some 'thing,'
some 'cause,' that if I removed it, I would be healed. I
faithfully took the medications my rheumatologist
prescribed, but I became obsessed with trying to
find a solution. Harry supported and helped me. He
kept his eyes and ears open for any new treatments
and possible cures. We heard somewhere that mercury in silver fillings could bring on arthritic symptoms, so I made an appointment with a good dentist.
Harry drove me over, and we had my silver fillings
replaced with porcelain. I didn't notice any immediate change in my condition, but I remained fairly sta-
ble for nearly a year. My prayers, my medications, all
were working.

"But my illness didn't allow me the ease of a routine pill that would make me feel better for the rest
of my life. There was always something changing, an
increase in pain, a new swollen joint, higher doses of
medications. The only thing that didn't change were
the frequent visits to the doctor.

"One morning I woke weak and dizzy. I could
hardly lift my Bible. My gums were bleeding. Harry
called my dentist and he recommended I go to an
oral surgeon who upon seeing me, suggested I get
off the methotrexate. My rheumatologist said
'absolutely not.' I became confused and frustrated,
frightened. What should I do? Insomnia tortured my
nights. I lost weight again. I was afraid to stop the
methotrexate, afraid of the pain. I didn't know what
to do. I became depressed. I felt like I was being
sucked into a deep, black hole.

"Harry kept encouraging me. He helped me with
anything I needed, but I knew he was at a loss too.

"Gina happened to call, as she sometimes did.

And although her relationship with us at that time was still strained, especially with her father, she told me that by studying Ayurveda and homeopathy she had been able to get herself off allopathic medicine, and if I were willing, she could try to help me."

Appreciation showed in Dee's face as she stroked Gina's shoulder, a softening in the muscles that held her mouth in a perpetual smile.

"It was a difficult time for both of us," Gina said, taking her mother's hand. "But something we had to go through. Even Dad, who struggled with his own demons, who still couldn't completely forgive me, hoped I could help. And so I made my way back into their life. But I made sure I set boundaries. I wanted to help my mother but refused to allow myself to be manipulated by their old ways.

"Studying Ayurveda, I became aware that my own healing had to do with more than herbs and a change of diet. A great part, both physically and mentally, was due to a change in attitude—not only in how I perceived people, things, issues, but how I allowed others to perceive me. I would help my mother, but not at the expense of my own health."

Aunt Dee seemed a little embarrassed that her daughter would speak with such force, such sureness, uncomfortable that perhaps her daughter didn't approve of the way she and Harry thought. But she answered placidly that she'd placed herself in her daughter's care.

"Weren't you afraid?" I asked.

A nervous giggle bubbled from Dee's throat. "A little, but Gina had the help of her instructors too."

I was impressed. Regardless of the circumstances, willingness is the first step to healing, courage the second. The time must have been right.

"Being in my care didn't mean stopping all the

medicine she'd been taking," Gina said. "That could put her system in shock. The plan was—is—to wean her away from heavy allopathic medications while treating her with Ayurveda and homeopathy. We began by changing her diet."

Gina named several food restrictions: red meat, seafood, anything too hot and spicy, too salty or sour, citrus fruit, persimmons, papayas, tomatoes, beets. The list was quite extensive. It was meant to help reduce the inflammation, the swelling, the fire in Dee's body.

"That's quite a restrictive diet," I said.

Dee nodded. "Gina said the choice was mine. I could stay with the drugs I was taking or try it her way. I continued with my medications and doctors' visits, but I started on Gina's food-restriction program."

"How did you do?" I asked.

"It wasn't easy. It took some getting used to, but I wanted to get better. I didn't want to hurt. If not eating certain foods would help, so be it."

A look of pain passed over her veiled eyes. A tiny tremor jerked at the corner where tears form. Had I not been looking directly at her in that very moment, I would have missed it. More lay locked away. I would have to be patient, listen, wait, then ask the right question.

"I also wanted her to go for treatment at the Maharishi Ayurveda Health Center," Gina said, "but first she needed to detoxify herself."

For the next few weeks, Aunt Dee followed Gina's instructions for detoxification. She took daily doses of ghee (clarified butter) every morning on an empty stomach. This would help the bowels to eliminate extra toxins. Before she showered in the morning, she did a self-body massage with sesame oil, to prevent the accumulation of psychological imbalances and help toxins to be eliminated through the skin. She avoided carbonated drinks and caffeine, instead drinking hot water and herbal tea. All her food was to be cooked and eaten in a quiet, settled environment. She did daily exercises as best she could, but mostly slow stretches, yoga sun salutations, and meditation.

Meditation? This interested me. Some religious people I have talked to believe meditation to be somehow evil, or related to black magic. My aunt, surprisingly, did not feel this way. She used meditation interchangeably with prayer. She meditated on passages of the Bible and used visualization to picture herself in beautiful places. It gave her pleasure, relaxed her.

"What did Uncle Harry think of all this?" I asked both Gina and Dee.

"He surprised me!" Gina said. "He accepted everything."

"He even went on the diet with me," Dee said.

Perhaps the diet helped my uncle as well, since it seemed he suffered from his own pent-up anger, something I suspected contributed to his fatal heart attack.

"When I felt mom was ready, I took her to the Maharishi's. It's local and she could go as an outpatient."

I was familiar with the Maharishi's, located just off Sunset Beach, a place where fragrances wafted through the air. The staff were of a gentle spirit and seemed to care about people, even if they were just coming for information. The treatment rooms were built around a peaceful courtyard full of lush plants and the sound of running water. Inside, the rooms were lit only by natural light, and any equipment used could not require electrical energy. It gave me tranquillity; I remembered thinking about how modern society was surrounded by mechanical technology, bombarding our bodies with its pulsing frequencies.

"They began by giving me herbal teas to drink," Aunt Dee said. "Then a light colon cleanse, and finally a massage." A spark of humor danced across her face. "At the time I was apprehensive. Two women entered the room in which I lay naked under a warm blanket. I don't like my body to be handled roughly. I'm not someone who seeks out massages, but Gina assured me this would help. I trusted my daughter.

"With one massage therapist on either side of me, they began to work. They moved softly, gently, evenly, each stroke the same as the other's. They mirrored each other. I closed my eyes and drifted to where I felt they were one person with many hands. I felt like I was floating, dreaming. When they finished, they left me to lie in the room, inhaling the beautiful fragrance that still lingered from the medicated oils they used. I never knew I could feel so good.

"The second time I went, I experienced much of the same, except my massage was done by only one person, and she followed it with a treatment called 'Shirodhara.' Quietly, I lay on my back. Above me hung a huge container with a narrow funnel. From the funnel, a steady stream of warm oil spilled onto the space on my forehead just between my eyes. From there, the oil oozed into my hair, dripped off, and collected in a basin around my head and shoulders. Again, I was apprehensive at first. Gina told me this would take anywhere from twenty to forty-five minutes. I was afraid it would be like a torture treatment, but the oil stream lulled me into a state of calmness, took my thoughts into a dreamland. I didn't worry about anything. I just let my mind go."

Gina smiled like a mother at her child.

"After that I made Mom surround herself with fragrances at home. Nice smelling oils, fresh flowers."

"Gina didn't know how much all her love and care meant to me," Dee said. "I knew then, in my heart, that even though she refuses to come to my congregation, she is a good person. She just doesn't understand how important my faith is to me. She didn't know what I had been through."

"I still don't know," Gina said.

Lapis Lazuli

When the gray-red of war frightens
and the world feels angry,
shape-shift,
float on clouds of lapis lazuli
listen to angelic choirs
hear the stories of old
create a magic
that strengthens
endures
and comes true.

Six

GINA'S EYES PLEADED with her mother. She had
wanted to know her stories for so long.

Aunt Dee glanced at me, as if not knowing what
to say, or where to begin with the memories that
seemed to be pressing forward with increasing
urgency.

"Were you always religious?" I asked, trying to
move her into a position from which she could focus
on a story.

"Yes," she said hesitantly. "My father—" she

paused for a long time. "Nita, Boetje, and I used to love to listen to him when he spoke in church."

She paused again. Closed her eyes. I could see them moving back and forth under the lids as if accessing files. When she opened them again, I knew she'd changed her mind. She would tell a different story.

"I came to love the Bible stories during the war when we were in the camp." She took a long, deep breath. Her eyelids fluttered and the muscles in her neck tightened, relaxed, tightened.

I thought for a moment that Gina's presence might be disturbing her mother, making it more difficult for her. But it soon became apparent that my aunt was digging deeper, reaching for memories she'd stuffed away. Her eyes became distant and she fumbled absentmindedly with the cuffs of her sweater. I could feel a heaviness settle in the room.

"The three of us were in the camp alone," Dee began. "Only Anna Yacobs, my father's friend, was there to help us. I was . . . I was seven when the Japanese found us hiding in the church building. We were there with the rest of the neighborhood. Maybe seventy-five or a hundred people. All of us were too frightened to stay in our homes, so we came to the church and barricaded the door with furniture. The Japanese were everywhere, and after four days they found us.

"They banged on the door, shouted for us to come out, or they would shoot their way in. Already they began to pry open the heavy doors. I can still hear the squeal of splitting wood, see the iron crowbar, hard and mean, as it was rammed through the door jam. Like an evil claw, it dug into the locks that protected us.

"We were trapped. There was nowhere to run or

hide. Everyone started to scream. Before we knew it, we were surrounded by soldiers—some were Indonesians armed with bamboo sticks. In my young mind, I couldn't understand why the once gentle natives turned against us Dutch people. Like many others, my father had given them a home, trusted them as our servants, provided for their food, and given them clothes, sometimes hand-me-downs from his own children. And they repaid us like this?

"I clung to Anna. Frightened, my insides shook, my insides hurt." Aunt Dee trembled and rubbed the swollen joints of her hands. She kept her eyes down; I knew she wasn't looking at her hands, but deeper, into a past she never wanted to remember. Now she could no longer stop the images from coming forth. She continued to rub, rub, rub her knuckles.

Gina looked at me, nervous, but with my eyes I soothed her, told her it was alright, that her mother just needed to gather herself before she could go on.

Aunt Dee began again, her voice an airy whisper.

"The soldiers lined us up against the wall with our backs to them. They told us to keep quiet or they would kill us. With my hands shaking, and my knees so weak they might collapse out from under me, I looked up at Anna. I saw her lips move in prayer, and I began to do the same thing. I prayed to be invisible. I didn't want them to see little me. I prayed God would help me, help us.

"Our prayers were answered. "They didn't shoot, but oh, what they put us through. Barefoot and only taking the clothes we wore, they marched us to a prison. A long walk on hot asphalt. At one point I saw a *grobak* [a wooden cart] piled high with bleeding, motionless bodies. I can't describe how that feels to a child. The horror of it. I wanted to scream, to run. I wanted my father. I wanted my mother. I wanted to cry. But I only walked on, staring at the back of Nita's head. Only staring at the movement of her brown hair, trying hard to remember when we used to play, and she'd let me brush it. I became too frightened to look around, frightened to breathe in the smell of death, sour, musty, and strangling. They're images you want to forget but never can.

"We were marched into a barbed wire compound, our housing a room stuffed with people. The beds were hard wood planks placed one above the other, bunk bed style. The lucky ones were those who got the top bed, away from the crawling insects and off the ground where people were forced to relieve themselves through holes in the wood flooring.

"The showers were no better. There were three. Outside. Surrounded by a half-meter-high wall, a large barrel of water with a scooping bucket was all we had. We were allowed to wash quickly, one after another, while the Japanese guards watched, some snickering and pointing.

"I don't know how long we were there, four or five days, maybe a week. Then we heard gunfire, people screaming. The Japanese soldiers ran from one place to another in the camp. British Gurkha troops burst through the camp gates. There was more shooting and Anna made us hide inside, lie down on the filthy floors. When the gunfire stopped, we slowly peeked out.

"The Japanese had fled. "We were free. But the Gurkha troops could not offer us any more than our freedom. No food. No safety. We were just free to go. But where? Our homes had been burned. Everything we had—our papers, photographs, furniture, clothes—everything had been destroyed. We were like beggars in the street, with our past in ashes.

"Thank God for Anna. She looked after us, found a large abandoned house where we could hide. We kept very quiet and stayed inside, sneaking outdoors only to relieve ourselves and to uproot food from nearby gardens. The Japanese were everywhere. It was only 1942. The war would not end for some time. Without a British stronghold in our area, there was no place we could go to be safe. Try as we might to stay invisible, within a few weeks we were captured again. This time the Japanese loaded us onto trucks. Crammed together were others of our church. Everyone was afraid, paralyzed with the helplessness and hopelessness of the situation.

"The camp they took us to this time was much bigger than the first. It had barracks, one next to the other. Many other women and children already milled within the gates of the prison. They formed a crowd and watched as we were unloaded off the trucks. I wondered how long they'd been here. Their faces were gaunt. No one smiled. They just stared, perhaps watching for acquaintances.

"Inside the barracks, palm mats lay one next to the other across the wood floor. Toilets were thankfully located at the other end of the camp. Again, we came with only the clothes we wore, and my little dress was filthy and needed patching. From somewhere I got a pair of short pants and a shirt. I looked like a little boy in them, but I didn't mind. Food came from the general kitchen. Day after day we were served the same food—half a coconut shell of rice and boiled vegetables. Sometimes we were lucky and the vegetables were not rancid.

"But God was good to us. Anna was a masseuse, and the Japanese eagerly called her for service. As payment she received extra food, which she shared with us. And there were also two of my father's servants. Free to roam, they magically discovered where we were and at times smuggled salted fish and beef jerky to Nita, Boetje, and me. We had to be very careful. We waited until the heat of day, then, pretending to play marbles, with stones of course, we inched close to the high fence which provided a spot of shade. Thinking little of us dirty children seeking comfort, the Japanese soldiers never suspected we received food forced under the fence or through a tiny hole.

"Others were not so lucky. I remember some boys were given the duty of carrying trash out to the dump. The Japanese were very strict about their rules, and if you didn't follow them, they delighted in an excuse to lock you up in a separate cell and beat you. Sometimes we heard the suspected offenders scream; sometimes it was their mothers whose screams we heard.

"That day, the boys apparently returned with food smuggled in from natives. Many natives did that for children. The Japanese discovered what they had done and immediately took action. The boys were dragged off. We never saw them again." Tears filled Dee's eyes. "They killed them I guess. I didn't allow myself to dwell on those ugly thoughts. You couldn't, or you'd die of fear.

"The camp was a frightening place. People became crazy there. They fought over standing in food lines, or for bath space and time. Sometimes Anna would get us up at four or five in the morning so we could use the toilets and get washed. I hated going to the toilets. They were smelly holes on the other side of the camp, and because of the distance and the people who became sicker and sicker, there was human excrement everywhere. In our bare feet we had to make our way through the smelly, fly-infested area, sometimes in the dark.

"One by one, people got weaker. Disease spread through the camp: malaria, dysentery, skin infections. The three of us, along with many more, became covered with boils and head lice. The only medicine we had was sulfur. Anna helped us smear it all over our bodies. In no time the camp was filled with bald, yellow-colored children.

"And at night there were screams that echoed through the dark. Children, adults having bad dreams, nightmares. I clung to Nita as we slept together on our palm leaf bed. And she clung to me. Sometimes it was to drive away our own nightmares, sometimes because the nights were cool, and our clothes were threadbare.

"We never knew what day it was, or for how long we were there. Our days ran into one another, were filled with walking back and forth, looking for something to do, something to occupy our time so we wouldn't have to think about what might happen to us. I often looked for mothers with infants and tried to help them. I love babies.

"I also made sure I visited Boetje daily. Sometimes I brought him his food. He had been placed in the infirmary because of his leg, but that didn't mean he got any extra food or special attention. In fact, the opposite. He lay with others dying of malaria, tuberculosis, or some other awful illness. Some patients made it out of the infirmary. Many didn't.

"Nita and I took our turn getting malaria, but Anna kept it quiet. She didn't want us to go into the infirmary. Seeing how they treated—or rather didn't treat—Boetje, she chose to take care of us herself. Daily she massaged our bodies believing that massage could heal, and it did. I don't remember how long I was sick, but eventually the malaria symptoms went away. I stopped shaking, could eat a little, and finally go out into the sun again.

"Boetje was less fortunate. The wound in his leg would not heal so he was kept in the infirmary, amidst the smell of uncontrolled bodies, the sound of unrelieved pain, and the fear of death."

Aunt Dee shook her head. "My visits with Boetje were short. It was too difficult, too ugly, too suffocating. Instead, I searched for other things to occupy myself. Sometimes I'd stop and listen to one of the boys who managed to bring in a guitar. The soldiers didn't seem to mind that he played. A few other boys had instruments too; and often, in the evening, they would give a little performance. Some of the older children had formed a small choir. I enjoyed listening to them. Their songs reminded me of the church, or the music my father would play at home.

"My father played the violin, you know. He had a job playing for the silent movies, but I loved it most when he played after dinner. The music was soft and

72 sweet, like an angel's. And my mother. They said Mother played the piano beautifully. I don't really remember. Sometimes I think I remember, but I'm not sure if it's my imagination, a dream, a memory, or something someone told me."

Aunt Dee became silent, thoughtful, as if trying to recall what it was she actually remembered.

I wanted to ask what had happened to her mother and father but couldn't bring myself to do it. I could see she was struggling. Her lips trembled, and her breathing had quickened. She lowered her glance so Gina or I couldn't see her tears. From the sleeve of her sweater, she pulled a tissue, blew her nose, dabbed her eyes.

Dee's voice cracked as she began again, but she made no mention of her father or mother.

"Shanne told us Bible stories in the camp. She was an old woman from our church. A beautiful woman with snow-white hair, blue eyes, and a gentle mouth that always had a smile for us children. Somehow she had managed to sneak a Bible into the camp, and in the evening she would tell us stories. We little ones especially gathered around, believing in the tales and in a time when all would be well again. We were all very sad when Shanne died. We missed her, and no one took over her story time."

Aunt Dee tilted her head toward the ceiling with her eyes closed. She seemed to be listening once again to the tales.

"I still remember them. They were good stories. They gave me hope. Shanne always finished with a Psalm: 'God is our shelter, our strength, ever ready to help in time of trouble. . . .'"[Psalm 46]

Aunt Dee took a deep breath. I looked at Gina.

Gina looked at me. We both looked at Dee. She was gazing straight ahead, her thoughts still apparently faraway. It was truly a miracle she'd survived at all. Stripped of childhood so young, yet able to draw strength from God by clinging to Bible stories—and maintaining a sanity which many lost.

I began to understand more clearly why Dee's faith was so important to her. What had saved her as a child, she clung to as an adult. The old ways gave some comfort.

"Phew. Gina ran a hand through her hair. I need something to drink. Anyone for tea?"

"I'll take one," I said, needing something warm to wrap my chilled fingers around, even though it wasn't cold out.

"I'll get it," Aunt Dee said.

"It's okay Mom, just sit. I'll do it." Gina walked around the counter into the kitchen, where she could still see and listen to us. "How did you get out of the camp?" She asked as she put the kettle on to boil.

"You didn't get out of a camp," Aunt Dee said. "You 'got out' when you died or the war ended." She laughed nervously, perhaps at her own sarcastic tone.

"One day someone ran through the camp. 'The war is over!' he shouted. We didn't believe him at first, but then others took up the cry. 'The war is over! The war is over!' And then we saw the camp leaders. Formerly so proud and arrogant, they looked dejected as they marched out, followed by American or English soldiers. I thought at first, we would be left homeless like before, but this time we were told the Red Cross would transport us the next morning.

"The war was over. It was 1945. I was ten. We

74 had been in the camp for nearly three years. I didn't know what to think or feel, but everyone seemed happy. 'The war is over. Things will be better now,' Anna told us.

"I tried to be happy but no longer knew what that meant. Perhaps it meant that I could be less afraid. I waited to see.

"The next morning, trucks took us to the train station. For three days we traveled by train, from Magelang, to Ambarawa, to Solo, and then Semarang. We were crowded into railway cars, all of us malnourished, sick, and hungry. The heat in the train felt suffocating, filled with heavy, bad smells, and not until we reached Semarang did we get any food.

"By then I was so hungry, but the food wouldn't stay in my stomach. Like many others, I vomited it up. We weren't used to rich food, anything seasoned, or large quantities. Maybe we weren't used to good, unspoiled food.

"Still weak, and some barely able to stand, we were loaded onto military trucks and taken to the harbor. There we were ordered to take an open steamboat to Jakarta. I'd never been on a boat, but I wasn't frightened. After all the confinements, it felt wonderful to taste the sea air, feel the cool breeze, and see the ocean swells.

"Boetje looked very pale and sickly, but now I sat with him all the time. Now that he was in the fresh air and away from the smell of death, I could hold his hand, kiss his cheeks. 'We're almost there,' I kept telling him. His hands were like ice, even under the hot tropical sun. The deep wound on his leg looked red, swollen, and painful. But there was nothing I could do except tell him we were almost safe.

"Upon arrival in Bandung, we were met by the

Red Cross. Many among us were taken immediately to the hospital. Boetje was one of them. There he received several blood transfusions. The Red Cross treated all our physical ailments. They freed us from lice and gave us medications for the boils, bites, and malaria. They fed us and gave us clean clothes, but no one asked us how we were on the inside. I had so much bottled up inside me, so much grief and pain I didn't know what to do with. I had to keep pushing my feelings down. How I longed for my father and my mother.

"It was here we also had to say good-bye to Anna. Dear sweet Anna, who loved me so much. I heard later she didn't live very much longer. They said tuberculosis. It's possible. Much of the camp years, she coughed and coughed, and sometimes I saw she coughed blood. But dear, sweet Anna. I wouldn't be alive today if it wasn't for her."

Gina brought the tea and handed her mother a cup—white porcelain with delicately painted violets. Aunt Dee took it, sipped. Her hands shook slightly. She smiled, licked her lips.

"Gina. She's so patient with me."

I took a cup of steaming tea. The aroma of cinnamon and cloves filled my nostrils and washed away the stench of the camp images. I wrapped my numb fingers around the wonderful warmth.

Green Tourmaline

Nature sends messages
of abundance,
season after season
plants sprout anew
their green tourmaline
blossoming into color,
even after drought or fire
nature restores
provides
for those willing
to open their innermost seed.

Seven

"I HAVE SOME cookies that will go nicely with this tea," Aunt Dee said, getting up from the couch. She came back from the kitchen with a plate of Dutch spice cookies. I remembered them from my own childhood. I picked one up and chewed happily.

"Mom, I had no idea," Gina said, when Dee sat back down. Her eyes were large with wonder, sympathy, and new understanding. "You never told Jeff or me."

"They're not stories you like to tell," Dee said, taking a cookie and placing it on the saucer of her teacup. "They're memories you want to forget. And for a while I thought I had. Then suddenly . . ." She looked at me. "With Harry dying . . . I don't know. The memories wouldn't leave me alone."

"Homeopathy could be responsible for some of that, too," Gina answered.

"I don't understand," I said. "I know only the basics of homeopathy." I understood that remedies were generally dilutions of natural substances from plants, minerals, and animals. I knew that the theory was like cures like, and the remedies specifically matched symptom patterns or "profiles" of illnesses. Administration of these dilutions acted to stimulate the body's natural healing response. But other than that, I didn't know how homeopathy worked.

"It's complicated. Homeopathy treats in layers," Gina explained. "Healing progresses in a reverse chronology, from the most recent maladies to the oldest. So, as I treat my mother for one thing, it may uncover another.

"When I first started working with my mother, she was having side effects from the methotrexate—insomnia, bleeding gums, and pain. I reduced her methotrexate and started her on grapeseed extract. After the first week, her pain decreased, her swelling subsided, and she slept better. I then added into her diet supplements of shark cartilage, glucosamine sulfate, and alfalfa.

"For a few weeks she remained pretty comfortable, but the pain returned sooner than I'd hoped. I then started her on *Rhus toxidendron*, a dilution made from poison ivy. This time the pain stabilized for several months before I had to change her medication."

"But I began to feel nervous and agitated," Aunt Dee interrupted. The frequent changes in medication worried me. I wanted to get better quicker, do more. Harry suggested we try Chelation treatments. I don't remember where he heard about them, but the next thing I knew we were driving to Tijuana, Mexico."

I was curious. I'd heard of chelation therapy, but knew little about it.

"The treatment itself doesn't take long," Aunt Dee said. "We sat in a big, airy room, with other people. Individual medications to remove heavy metals and toxins from the blood were given intravenously. Harry took treatments too. He was experiencing problems with his prostate at the time and told me since he had to be there for me, he might as well try to help himself. The medication usually took no longer than an hour to drip in, but the required blood and urine tests needed to be done the day before, so it always turned into an overnight excursion."

I had only heard secondhand stories about treatments in Mexico, and they were always less than savory. They told of dirty facilities, rude doctors, and unfriendly nurses who spoke only Spanish, but Aunt Dee painted a very different picture. She explained that the treatments were all handled very professionally. The doctors all spoke English, were very friendly, the rooms were clean, and all the equipment brand new.

Initially, she didn't ask what medication dripped into her veins, but after a few weeks she became curious. She learned that her medication consisted mostly of vitamins, plus "something to ease" the arthritis. The doctor named a substance she didn't understand, making her nervous, and so she asked to have it excluded from her intravenous.

The doctors complied.

She and Harry went for treatment weekly, then bimonthly. After two months Aunt Dee stopped, claiming her veins could not hold out, and the trip made her nervous.

"Did the treatments help?" I asked.

Aunt Dee shrugged. "I don't know. I didn't feel bad while taking them, nor did I feel better when I finished with the treatments. I don't feel any different since I stopped, either. Who knows what works?"

Aunt Dee placed her cup and saucer in her lap. She broke off a piece of cookie and put it in her mouth, chewing slowly.

"Chronic illnesses like rheumatoid arthritis are like that," Gina said. "Very difficult to treat, and recovery is very subtle. Everyone has bad days, but when you have arthritis you always think it's the illness. Curing and healing are two very different principles. All I wanted for my mother was for her to have relief from pain, for her to be able to live a normal life. But Mother's case was far too complex for my training. It takes years to fully understand homeopathy. Fortunately, my professors offered their help. One of them examined Mother with me and prescribed *Nat muriaticum* and *Pulsatille*.

"I believe that's when changes really started happening," Gina said. "Issues of fear, grief, dreams, desires came to the surface, but they were images she wouldn't talk about."

"The black magic and life with Aunt Erika?" I asked Aunt Dee.

"Yes, and those of the camp." She looked into the teacup she held in her lap, took a deep breath. "Those and . . ." She stopped.

"And?" I prompted, but she didn't go on. She only looked into her cup, lost in the golden liquid.

There were things she still couldn't speak of. Gina knew this too. I could tell by the way she held her breath, waiting for her mother to say more. But Aunt Dee didn't continue. Gina and I exchanged a quick glance.

"About how long ago did these images start coming forth?" I coaxed.

"Maybe a couple years," she answered. "I started to write, but I just couldn't write it all."

"Harry couldn't help you?" I asked, thinking she meant, her hands would become too painful with the effort of writing, but that wasn't it.

"I tried to talk to him about it," Dee said. "But he didn't want to hear about those times. He'd start telling me about his problems at work, the customers who nagged, the overload he couldn't refuse. I hated to burden him. I knew he was having a lot of stress. It showed in his behavior. More and more, he would lose his temper. Our grandson, Rex, became afraid of him, didn't want to come over very often. When he did come, I'd explain to him that his grandfather was just tired, not to take his anger personally. Gina was the only one I could talk to."

"But she didn't tell me these stories," Gina said. "Mom talked about how she always wanted to be a good grandmother, how important she thought family and religion were, how she had malaria as a child, was possibly exposed to tuberculosis, was an orphan, but she didn't tell me the stories. I knew memories were bubbling to the surface. There were days when she looked on the verge of tears, and she admitted to being afraid but wouldn't tell me of what.

"I had to keep changing her medications. Over the course of the next year, I gave *Streptococcin* to remove the bad effects of sicknesses suppressed by modern antibiotics. I gave *Tuburculinum* to remove symptoms of tuberculosis exposure. I gave *Carsinossin* to remove the symptoms of pain caused by personal history. And each time, we were able to cut back just a little more on her allopathic medication."

"What did your doctor think of all this?" I asked.

"He was fine with it as long as I came to him for checkups," Aunt Dee answered. "He didn't really know what we were doing. We didn't go into detail with him. I don't think he wanted to know."

"What about your son, Jeff? Where was he all this time? Could you talk to him?"

"Oh no, no, no," Aunt Dee said, shaking her head. Jeff's a good man, smart too. In many ways he's like Harry—handy around the house, a loving husband, a good son. But I can't talk to him about these things. He might get upset. I don't want to see him angry."

Chrysocolla

Like the blue green
layers of needle-like
crystals
that make chrysocolla,
connection between hearts
opens the door
to emergence,
recognition that one
is part of the whole.

Eight

I LIKED GINA. I wanted to know her better. I thought she could give me more insight into her mother, a way of further helping Aunt Dee.

I gave Gina a call, and we arranged to meet at her house.

Unlike her mother's perfectly manicured home, Gina's felt wild and carefree. Her garden was a tangle of colorful shrubs and flowers, scattered randomly behind a low wooden fence with bright tulips painted on it. Inside, her home was equally vivid. Walls in royal blue, chartreuse, and red. Hardwood floors, a black rug, and red couch. Incense filled the air. On one wall she'd draped a batik. On another hung a Tibetan *tanka* (religious painting). Though crazy with color and practically vibrating with life and energy, the place felt warm, and womblike.

We drank iced herbal tea as we talked.

"I can't help feeling your mother is holding something back," I told Gina.

"I'm surprised she's told you—us—as much as she has. She never would have done that while my dad was alive."

"Why not? He wanted to see her well."

Gina crossed her legs beneath her batik sarong. Her feet were bare, her toes, painted a deep burgundy that matched her fingernails and the color of her hair. She tapped her fingers on the table.

"You didn't know my father very well, did you?" she asked.

I thought about it. "I guess not. I only saw him at family reunions, or when he and your mom visited my parents, and I happened to be there."

"He was a very proud man," Gina said. "He didn't like anyone to know anything 'bad' about our family. He tried to control everything. He even told me he wouldn't fix my car if I didn't cut my son's hair to the length he, my dad, thought appropriate. He did the same to my brother and me when we were younger. Tried to make us do things his way. He withheld love or "things" if we didn't do as he said. I fought him. I could be just as stubborn as he. Jeff became quiet, bottled up his frustration, stayed out of my dad's way."

She tapped her fingers again on the table.

"Did Mom tell you I warned him?"

"What do you mean?"

"That I warned my dad about his heart?"

"No," I said. "She didn't mention it."

"A week before my dad died, I was practicing my kinesiology. When I came to the area of his heart, I had an odd feeling. I muscle-tested him. He tested weak. I told him he should get his heart checked out. But he said, 'what for?' He felt fine, and he didn't like doctors. He was a bullheaded man.

"Your mom seemed to handle your dad okay. She seemed happy with him."

"Oh ya," Gina nodded. "My mom was. She was willingly controlled by my dad."

I stared at Gina; her beautiful green eyes stared right back.

"It fits doesn't it," I said. "It's a pattern of your mother's. In the camp she's controlled. At Aunt Erika's she's controlled. With your father, his control is comforting. Same thing with her religion. The rules are comfortable to her. She needs guidelines. She's always been told what to do."

Gina blinked. "You're right!"

"This is the first time she is in control of her own life," I said.

We sat in silence for a while, each of us pondering what all this meant. Gina, I'm sure, was putting this in a context of her next treatment. I, on the other hand, was wondering how I could break that pattern.

Moonstone

With the soft, white light
of a moonstone
imperfections are transformed,
veils are lifted
fears released
and the true essence
of the inner world
shines on the outer.

Nine

BY JUNE, SPRING had tiptoed into Summer, turning the weather unusually warm. Mornings, Aunt Dee threw open her windows and sliding doors to let in the cool air. By afternoon she'd close them all, pull down some of the window shades, and use portable fans to move the air. The air conditioner aggravated her joints.

As we sat in the kitchen with glasses of water and apricots picked fresh from her tree, she told me shyly of another dream.

"I'm sitting alone and suddenly see a bright yellow mountain before me. It has multiple jagged peaks. The right side of the mountain is yellow, the left side is black. Someone I can't see tells me, 'climb the mountain,' so I try. I embrace the whole mountain, both the yellow and the black, and inch up the slippery side.

"Isn't it silly how dreams make no sense?" she said. "Imagine climbing a mountain that way. I'd have to be a giant." She gave that nervous laugh of hers.

"Did you get to the top?" I asked.

"I got half way up before I woke up."

She looked like a little girl who had just brought me some lovely morsel. And she had. Unconsciously, she knew her dream was a powerful one, but her faith would not allow her to believe in it. Nonetheless, she'd presented the image for me to work with, that I would give it words she could understand and accept. Several obvious associations came immediately to mind. Mountains have height and verticality, traditionally masculine symbols, that can reflect the sexual aspects of masculinity as well as outward expressions of assertiveness. Mountains can be symbols of spiritual elevation and commu-nion with blessed dieties, or represent triumph over seemingly insurmountable obstacles. I wanted, how-ever, to give my aunt a chance to make her own asso-ciations.

"What do you think it means?" I asked.

She hesitated, perhaps not wanting to answer because that might indicate her belief in dreams.

I waited.

"I don't know," she said, finally. "It's just a dream."

I tried another approach. "Do you think telling me your stories has helped you? I mean, do you feel better now that you've told someone the secrets you've kept hidden for so long?"

"Yes."

Her eyes told me she did feel relief. She blinked, looked away from me, then back. There was something else. We had gone all the way back to the time she'd entered the camp, when she was seven. But what had happened to her parents? How did they die? Had she seen something too awful for words?

"Maybe the dream is telling you, you're climbing closer to God by accepting your past, by embracing the dark with the light," I said. "Perhaps you are stronger now, have more confidence in yourself. Perhaps you can still climb higher."

I paused, letting her think about that.

After a moment she said, "Ya, huh?"

I nodded. "Confidence to go on with your life and . . . your stories." I took her hand, held it, examined the nodules. They were not red or warm. She did not flinch at my touch. "There's still more, isn't there?" I asked, meeting her eyes.

Her breath caught in her chest, then slowly, she exhaled. She looked at me, but past me, taking on that faraway reflectiveness. I could feel emotions rising from her depths. I could feel her struggle with nightmares from another lifetime, visions that never left her alone, that shouted at her, ate at her, and festered in her body.

She opened her mouth to speak but could not.

"It's okay," I said. "You're safe now."

She sat back into the wooden slats of the kitchen chair, sliding her hand from mine. She picked up an apricot, rolled it in her hand. Several more minutes passed, then she began. Her voice was barely a whisper.

"My parents died before we went into the camp," she said, and stopped.

I didn't know how to encourage her further. For a moment I thought she wouldn't say any more, that she'd gone back as far as she was willing or able to; but she began again.

"When the Japanese invaded our city early in 1942, they organized regular patrols to be on the lookout for anyone who appeared even slightly unnative. The Dutch, the Australians, Indonesian mixes were dragged off to camps.

"We lived in a small but cozy house not far from the *kampung* [native section]. A barbed wire fence ran the length of the kampung to discourage thieving natives from coming into our part of town. But when the Japanese patrolled our area, we would often slip under the fence to run and hide behind the grass huts.

"Boetje had to be the most careful. He was the fairest of the three of us. We had to rub him down with *arang* [wood-charcoal] to hide his light brown hair and to darken his face.

"One day, a troop of Japanese soldiers took us by surprise. We didn't have a chance to get away. They kicked in our door. My father tried to protect us, but there were too many of them. They punched him, kicked him until he fell to the floor in pain, and then they kicked him some more."

Aunt Dee kept her eyes on the smooth skin of the apricot. Ran the soft part of her thumb over a tiny sunspot on the fruit. Back and forth went her thumb, as if wanting to ease away the bruise. Her lower lip trembled, but she found the courage to continue.

"Nita and I were holding on to each other. We were too frightened to make a sound. When my father could do nothing more than writhe in pain, the soldiers dragged him to their truck. Another two Japanese soldiers grabbed Boetje. He was screaming and crying. They threw him into the truck where he clung to my father.

"There was nothing Nita or I could do. I was not quite seven, Nita ten." A tear spilled from Dee's eye and fell to her lap. "It was the last time we saw our father alive. As the truck drove away, Nita and I just stood there afraid to breathe, afraid to move. Afraid. So afraid.

"Afraid, afraid," Aunt Dee repeated. Her eyes darted about, not seeing me, living again in her past. Her shoulders pulled up and inward as she dropped the apricot and wrapped her arms around herself. She shivered, then let her hands slide slowly to her lap. "To this day I can see those khaki-colored uniforms, hear my father's groans, see my brother's face. The fear." Her voice cracked.

"Anna Yacob found Nita and me still clinging to each other. She took us in immediately, told us everything would be alright. She kept us occupied by working in the garden, harvesting what was ripe, and planting new vegetables—yams, corn, peanuts. Some days we woke up to find that our garden had been raided. 'Natives,' Anna told us with bitterness. 'Native thieves,' but that didn't stop us from harvesting what was left and continuing to plant more.

"We cooked on wood charcoal stoves because

we had no utilities. Our water came from a well infested with worms, and our light from coconut oil lamps."

Aunt Dee took a deep breath. "I can barely remember the time when I had a happy family." A sudden smile pulled at her lips. "There was a time, though, when I dressed in pretty clothes, ate whatever I wanted, played happily. I remember going on walks with my mother and father, Boetje and Nita. My father would take the little boats he had carved to the nearby pond, and with hollow reeds and papaya seeds we made a game of shooting at the little boats. He was so creative with his games. And mother had such a beautiful laugh.

"And then there were the evenings when we would sit and listen to my mother and father play music. She played the piano, he the violin. I'm not sure I really remember those nights. It's more like imagining I remember. A happy, carefree life with no fear is something I have to pretend I can feel. It was so long ago, and I was so young." Aunt Dee looked down at her hands and sighed. "Still, I would have liked to play the piano . . .

"My mother died when I was four. Cancer, they said, but what did that mean to me? One day she was home, the next day she was gone. They took her to the hospital, and I never saw her again. I missed her terribly and cried daily, begging my father to take me to see mama. But he never did. Months, perhaps a year, passed before he told me she'd died and I would never see her again.

"My father tried his best to raise us properly. He looked at our school work, took us to church, made time to play with us. He took us on walks in tropical gardens, where colors danced about us, and fragrances floated in heavy afternoon humidity. The roses were especially strong, and when a soft breeze blew, it was as if roses followed me. Roses still remind me of my mother. She always smelled of flowers. I used to brush my mother's long flower-scented hair and wrap it around me like a shawl. She let me play like that.

A furrow creased Aunt Dee's forehead.

"As an adult, you have more insight into your past." She said it as though she'd just become aware of that advantage. "I guess my mother was never strong."

I could actually see the sadness spread over her.

"I had so little of family joy," she said.

She swallowed hard.

I knew she was trying to form the words for the rest of her story.

"Perhaps a week after the Japanese took my father, they returned Boetje to us. He was thin, with dark circles under his eyes, and he had the ugly gash on his leg that would someday kill him. At night he cried out, woke with nightmares, but he didn't talk about what had happened in the camp. All we knew was that our father was dead. We had no one. No one except Anna.

"Anna watched after us. So did our servants. The ones that stayed loyal to us because there was nowhere for them to go either. At least with us, they had land where they could grow food.

"But one day . . . our houseboy called to me. He was nineteen or twenty, a man actually, but he did the work of a houseboy—sweeping the floors, running errands for my father . . . when he was alive.

"We were all outside, working in the garden, playing. The houseboy told me he wanted to show me something. I followed him into the house. I had no reason not to trust him."

Aunt Dee's hands shook. She tried to hold them still by squeezing them together but with little success.

"There was no reason for me not to trust him," she repeated, her eyes welling up. "My father had always been good to him." Her voice quivered. The veins in her neck pulsated.

I could already guess what happened. I shook on the inside myself. I sensed her pain, her fear. The shame she'd carried all these years was overwhelming. What had happened to her were not things women, young or old, ever told anyone about, and especially not in those days.

A few tears trickled down her face as she spoke.

"He pulled me into a room. Shut the door. He pushed. Forced. Slapped me to the floor. His hands. Tight over my mouth. Couldn't breathe. Couldn't scream. Frightened, so frightened. I struggled. Everything became dark. The air, heavy. He was angry. Why was he angry with me? Couldn't breathe. Couldn't breathe. I didn't know what was happening. He ripped at my panties. . . And then there was pain. So much pain. Again and again and again . . ."

Aunt Dee covered her face. I expected a flood of tears, relief from a secret held so long, but there was nothing so dramatic. She kept her face covered until she'd controlled her rising emotions. Then, with red eyes and a quivering voice, she continued.

"I felt dizzy, like I had fallen into a great black pit. I thought maybe I would die. And then, he was gone. I didn't move or open my eyes for a long time. I just lay there crying, my breath stuck inside me. Something awful, something dirty, had happened to me. Why?"

I got up and put my arms around my aunt. A few tears came, but crying uncontrollably was not her way.

She patted my hand. "I'm okay."

I sat back down in my chair and held her hands across the table. They were cool and slightly moist.

"Did you tell anyone?" I asked.

She shook her head.

"Not Anna?"

She shook her head again. "Not Anna. Not even Nita."

"But didn't you need to see a doctor?" I could not begin to imagine a child of seven enduring such an assault and then not receiving any medical care. It went against all human sensibilities.

"I became very sick," Aunt Dee said. "I couldn't eat, became pale, easily frightened, and cried a lot. When Anna noticed my underpants were blood-stained she took me to someone. A woman. Not a doctor, maybe a midwife. She examined me, but nothing could be done. And I said nothing of what had happened. I couldn't. For weeks I continued to have pain, nightmares, and woke up in pools of sweat.

"And even when God helped me heal physically, I could not forget. I became suspicious and frightened of people, especially men. And to make matters worse, the war was escalating and fear took on a whole new meaning. Planes flew overhead daily. I could hear bombs exploding, feel the earth tremble. Sirens sounded and we'd all run for the bomb shelters.

"The shelters were musty, damp, underground

dugouts. When it rained they filled up, and we'd have to wade knee-deep in water infested with swarming insects, worms, and snails. Months of hiding like this in the dark waters, sometimes for hours, was what made Anna and the others decide to barricade ourselves in the church.

"And shortly after that we were captured by the Japanese." She took a huge breath. "The rest you know."

She took hold of her glass of water, seemed to check herself before she lifted it to her mouth. When she placed the glass back on the table, she ran her fingers around its rim.

"I've never told that to anyone. Not even Harry."

Malachite

High on the bluff
wind echoes through
the caves
blows away shadows
broadens views
allows for clear vision
of the sky above
as well as
the sea below.

Ten

REMARKABLY, AUNT DEE did not dwell on the rape. Once she'd let out her deepest secret, and we talked about how it wasn't her fault or her shame to carry, she felt hugely unburdened. It became easier for her to speak. She filled in details about her past and began to draw impressions of her life. She could mourn her losses, and for the first time, saw her strengths.

The more she told me, the more she threw herself into life. I could see the changes. No longer did a dark vapor seem to shroud her. A new lightness enfolded her, and she no longer held her body so rigidly. Her eyes had lost their dullness, and for the first time in my life, I saw her eyes dancing and sparkling as they must once have done as a young child.

By the end of June and into July, Aunt Dee had three new paintings—all nature scenes. One depicted an Arizona landscape. Massive rocks glowed reddish orange in sunrise, or sunset. She'd managed to capture the depth and majesty of those rough cliffs. Yet there was also a skeletal quality to the painting, a stripping to the bare bones—all very different from her first flowers, where sadness weighed heavily on the landscape.

I found her choice of subject matter fascinating, since rocks are so symbolic of stability and sturdiness. Rocky, mountainous terrain, offers a vantage point from which we gain new perspectives. And certainly my aunt was looking at her life with a new perspective.

Another painting featured a Hawaiian coast line. Giant volcanic mountains, dark and purple, plunged to the sea below. The cloudy sky had streaks of gold in it, and for some reason this reminded me of the dream where she was climbing the mountain. But to that symbol of masculine strength, she had added the ocean, a symbol of the womb, mother, woman. A dynamic force, as constantly in transition as the subconscious mind.

The last painting pictured a single-room hut with a red roof. Nestled on the side of a rugged mountain, the hut lay on the edge of a meadow in a patch of sun. I was encouraged, for meadows are places of abundant life.

"That one is for Gina," she said. "I don't know what I would do without her." Aunt Dee stood back and admired her work. "She helped so much. She's done more for my arthritis than any doctor, and she was immediately there for me when Harry died."

"We haven't talked much about Harry's death," I said.

"No," she almost whispered. "We haven't."

"Would it be uncomfortable for you to talk about him?"

"I don't think so."

I settled myself more comfortably on the couch. I took a moment to think of what I might want to ask her.

"Did Uncle Harry's passing cause your arthritis to flare up?"

She gave me a puzzled look.

"Surprisingly not," she said—and really did seem surprised.

"Gina took immediate care of me," she said. "Everything happened so fast that day."

Aunt Dee's eyes took on that familiar distant look. I could feel her wanting to clarify in her own mind why her arthritis had not flared up.

"Harry told me he didn't feel good," she began. "He said he had some kind of indigestion and wanted to lie down for a while. When I checked on him only a few minutes later, he wouldn't answer me. I tried to move him, sit him up, but he was too heavy. His lips were turning blue and his face had become a pasty gray. I called the paramedics immediately, then Gina.

"The hospital is close-by. The paramedics were

here in less than five minutes. So was Gina. The paramedics jumped into action the minute they saw Harry. They jabbed him with needles, pumped his chest, breathed into his mouth. They brought out round paddles that jolted his body. When I saw his body arch, I turned away. I couldn't watch. Gina gave me some kind of homeopathic medication. 'For the shock,' she said. I took it.

"They transported Harry to the hospital almost immediately. Gina and I followed in her car. When we got to emergency room they rushed him into an examining room. We stayed in the waiting room. Made phone calls. Waited some more. We waited a long time.

"Time crept by slowly. Jeff and his wife, Ena, arrived. Some of our close friends came, sat with me, waited, waited, waited.

"Harry was dead. Even before the doctor came out to tell us, I knew. I could feel it.

"Gina took me home. She took care of me, gave me *Ignatia*. She said it was for the 'grief of losing a loved one.' Then she gave me *Arnica* to help heal the pain in my back. I strained it trying to lift Harry. Gina, her husband, Joby, and Rex stayed with me that night and for many nights after.

"It must have been the medication Gina gave me that kept my arthritis from flaring up." Aunt Dee shook her head. "Gina lost her father, but her thoughts were all for me. It's hard to believe he's gone. To walk into my house by myself felt so different, so lonely. But it's better now," she added quickly.

"Maybe his spirit still watches over you," I said.

She smiled. "You sound like Gina. Gina was convinced that Harry's spirit was in the house. She said she could feel him." Aunt Dee sighed, the sigh of a

tolerant parent. "The Bible speaks of the dead as conscious of nothing. They are in God's memory. God
provides us with a wonderful hope to see our loved
ones again on earth, but under very different circumstances, the Resurrection hope."

Still smiling, she looked at me with some new
glint in her eye. She seemed to be teasing me, knowing that I knew she was up to something.

"I've decided to go to Holland in August," she con-
fessed.

"Alone?"

"Yes," she glanced down, then back up at me.
"I've told Harry's family, and they said not to worry.
They would be there to meet me."

I wanted to cry. This was a giant step. I was as
proud of her as a mother who witnesses her baby
jump into the water and swim for the first time.

"I'm taking Harry's ashes," she said.

"What are you going to do with them?"

"I don't know yet."

Fluorite

Shades of violet and purple
line walkways
offer peaceful stillness
soothe chaos
bring recognition
of life's purity
cleanse
and brighten the new day
to restore faith
in Self.

Eleven

SEPTEMBER, ALONG WITH all its heat, finally came. I could hardly wait to meet with my aunt. She'd been gone for a month, and then two more weeks passed before we could arrange to get together. Although in Dee's absence, Gina had given me reports that her mother was doing well, having a great time, and not having any problems with her arthritis, I was eager to hear Dee's stories. I wanted to know how she had fared on her first trip alone.

When she greeted me at the door, years seemed to have washed away. Light danced in her eyes, and—she wore a lovely, excited smile—a real smile, not one to hide pain. This one bubbled with news. She threw her arms around me in a tight hug even before I was completely inside.

"It's good to see you," she said, stroking my arm as if I were her favorite pet.

"You had a good trip?" I laughed.

"Oh yes, come sit down. I'll show you pictures."

The house was not cool, although pleasant enough. She had two floor fans going, and every few seconds one of them blew softly on me.

"Is it too warm for you?" she asked.

"I'm fine." And I was. We get so spoiled using air conditioners when all we really need is to move the air around a little.

"A new painting already?" I said, noticing the easel.

She smiled shyly. "I had to paint it the moment I got home."

Again her style had changed. In the foreground flowed a river, turbulent and fast moving, according to the strokes; but both sides of the river were lined with delicate, happy-looking flowers. A bright and sturdy bridge, close to the focal point of the painting, crossed over the river and led directly to a cottage, with trees and a windmill off to one side. It was a cheery picture, and reminded me of a fairy tale.

"I like it. Your trip must have been good."

"Wonderful. You'll never believe."

She pulled out a picture album and opened it to the first page. It didn't surprise me that she already had her pictures organized. She tapped her finger on the plastic sleeve.

"This is Harry's brother and sister. And this is ..." She spoke like a small child hurrying to recite every part of her adventure.

"Harry's family told me stories of when Harry was little. They said he was a clever, creative young boy, one who would always figure a way out of a problem. He was a hard worker and always determined to have his way." She looked up from the album. "He was like that all his life. Determined to have his way. But I needed that, then."

I understood. I believe we have choices, but we are always where we need to be in life, even if we don't like it.

"This is John with his family," she said, returning to the album. "He said Harry became the head of the household at an early age, and he admired his older brother like a father. And Christien, Harry's sister, said sometimes he was too much a father, and everyone laughed."

Aunt Dee had shared some of her own stories. She told the family how she remembered going on Harry's motorbike. Together with their friends, Rudy and Neeltje, the four of them would motor to Maribaja, Bogor, Poentjak, Lembang. They were beautiful places, gardens of tropical plants and colorful birds. For hours the four of them would walk around, breathe in nature, and picnic on *pisang* and *ketella goreng* (fried banana and fried cassava). Sometimes they would bring their dinner of rice and chicken *saté* and enjoy the view overlooking Bandung as they talked late into the night.

"They were wonderful memories of Indonesia," Aunt Dee said. "Memories I'd forgotten until now."

She told stories of Harry, later, when they were in

Holland. How, with the children, they'd gone on camping trips through Germany, Austria, Switzerland, and Italy. Harry's younger brother also remembered the trips. He had gone with them, as well as another couple, and their three children. They took two cars but camped together.

"Those were marvelous times." Aunt Dee smiled. "We would swim in lakes or sit in the sun, play games in the evening, and sleep in tents. We took the kids camping when we came to America too. Yosemite, Lake Shasta, the Grand Canyon. But those times we took a motor home. We'd come a long way from Harry's motorbike."

"But I didn't just visit Harry's family."

She had contacted her side of the family as well, family she had not seen in over fifty years. She had always done things Harry's way, she explained. Gone only where Harry wanted to go, seen only friends Harry wanted to see. She never complained. There was no reason to, but now things were different. She could do what she wanted, see who she wanted. And so she did. She saw cousins from her side of the family who were beyond happy to see her again. And they, too, exchanged stories and came to new discoveries.

Aunt Dee remembered that before her father was taken prisoner, one of Anna Yacob's grandchildren had lived with them. Wally was his name, and he was just two. His father had already been captured by the Japanese, and his mother had become emotionally unstable. Dee was excited to have a little baby in the house, a little brother. She was only six herself, but she liked babies, and the job of watching Wally fell to her.

One day while they were sitting beneath the avocado tree, Wally began to shiver uncontrollably. Little Dee carried Wally into the house and took him immediately to Anna. By evening Wally was burning with fever, vomiting. Dee helped Anna mix water with *daun ingoe* and lime, a concoction of leaves the natives used to lower fever, but nothing helped.

Wally died of malaria within a few days.

Together the family made his coffin. Dee helped pad the inside with white cloth stuffed with *waringin* leaves. She, her sister, and brother gathered flowers from the gardens, especially the gardenias and the double jasmines that smelled like heaven. They sprinkled them over his little coffin as it was lowered into the ground.

She wiped a tear from her eye as she retold the story to me.

"I love babies," she whispered.

I took a deep breath, knowing that, having unlocked the doors, my aunt would have many more memories emerge. I had come to understand that this was a woman who loved life. Who had always loved children. Who had watched the suffering of many without being able to help. I understood why her own children meant so much to her, and Rex's birth. And I also understood why expressing that love had been difficult, perhaps even painful. She had lost so many she'd loved.

Her attention fell back to the album, and she turned the page slowly.

"This is Heide, right?" I said. I had never met her, but my mother had pictures of her and visited her on trips to Holland. "And this is Marie?"

Aunt Dee nodded. "I haven't seen either one of

them for fifty years. We had wonderful visits," she said and laughed. "I finally got to tell Marie I was jealous of her as a little girl."

"Why?"

"When Marie and her family came to visit at Aunt Erika's, Marie would sit in her father's lap. The lap that I wanted to cuddle in. I missed my father so much. She and I laughed about it, but we also cried. It was good to be able to tell her how I felt."

We flipped through more pictures, while Aunt Dee made comments on places and people, the weather, her health—all good, all wonderful. Finally we came to the last three. They showed a grave site. A beautiful grave in the midst of a flower garden.

"That's Harry's mother's, Sitie Katminah."

"It's so pretty with all those flowers," I said.

"In Holland, the graveyards are different than here," Dee explained. "The yards are like parks. Green walkways line flower beds where the gravestones lie." She paused. "I put some of Harry's ashes with his mother. Some I kept for myself, some I gave to Gina, and some to Jeff. Jeff's already scattered his ashes in the ocean just off San Clemente. He took his boat out and found just the right place. Harry would be pleased."

Tiger's Eye

Life is full of
pasts and futures
that rip and claw
spiraling us into worry.
Be more conscious
of the hum of voices,
the soundless night,
the tiger's eye . . . gold
in rich planting soil
that sees through seasons
and reminds there is no
reason for impatience.

Twelve

THE FOLLOWING WEEK when I arrived at Aunt Dee's, I found the energy very different. Jeff and his wife, Ena, had temporarily moved in. They were planning to buy a house closer to Jeff's mother, and as luck would have it, their home in San Clemente sold more quickly than expected. For convenience, they moved in with Aunt Dee while they kept looking.

As I entered the house, I immediately noticed the coolness of air conditioning. The fans, usually whirring with a comforting hum, stood quietly in the corner.

"You've turned on the air conditioner?"

"Jeff and Ena get too warm," Aunt Dee whispered.

"But what about you?"

"I put on a sweater."

She laughed, one of those nervous little laughs. I sensed she knew what I was thinking—she was not standing up for herself. And the idea that I might think less of her for it made her self-conscious. She didn't know, I could only admire her.

"They put most of their things in storage," she said.

Only then did I notice the dining table crowded in the space beside the sliding glass door, and her easel folded up and placed against the wall. There were lots of little knickknacks and brick-a-brac not belonging to my aunt: crystal figurines, vases, framed pictures.

"These are wonderful." I indicated the pictures that now hung on the wall by the kitchen. One of them showed Aunt Dee and Uncle Harry on a motorbike with the palm trees of Indonesia behind them. Another was a small portrait of the two of them. It must have been taken early on in their courtship. They were both so young and dreamy looking.

"Jeff brought them." Aunt Dee said, and wondered aloud why she didn't have them there in the first place.

"You're both so young," I remarked. It suddenly

dawned on me that perhaps only now could she comfortably have reminders of the past around her. Reminders of Indonesia, and of Uncle Harry.

Sudden barking made me turn to the backyard door. Two Dalmatians stared at me, their brown eyes shining in the sun.

"Dogs?"

She wrinkled her nose. "They're good dogs."

I walked closer to the door, to get a better look. They were fine, healthy animals. Large for Dalmatians, and with husky bodies. Then I noticed that Aunt Dee's purple flowers along the hedge to the pool had been trampled; the kitty place mat was gone, and in its stead were two large metal feeding dishes. Not too small a pile of droppings had been left on the walkway to the pool.

"Jeff or Ena will clean that up later," she said. "They're good about not letting me do their work. They even try to bring food in so I don't have to cook."

There was more barking as I walked away from the door and set my briefcase next to the couch.

"Do you get along with the dogs?"

She nodded. "But I get goose bumps. I can't help it. They scare me, especially when Jeff brings them into the house. But what can I do?"

My first reaction was that she'd had a relapse. I wanted her to continue to be a "take charge" woman—but then I thought of the way I am with my own children. I know how it is. I don't always like what my kids do, but they are my kids so I tolerate it and don't say much, especially if it's temporary. I don't like to make waves either. It is important to know when to speak up, and when the victim personality is making you overly sensitive. I imagined, however, that Jeff knew nothing of his mother's fear of dogs, or why she liked a clean, uncluttered look.

"It must be difficult to have your routine upset," I said.

"It's not so bad. Jeff does so much for me. Anything that needs fixing, he fixes. He's like his father that way. He likes everything to operate perfectly."

I was happy for her but also concerned. I hoped Jeff wouldn't take over her life. He might believe he was required, as her son, to fulfill the role of his father to do what he thought she needed, not ask what she wanted.

Orange Calcite

Fulfillment doesn't come from wealth
or obligations carried
out for others,
it comes
on grateful smiles
of those comforted and
in orange calcitian eyes
of a stray animal
fed
by a singing heart
and a joyful touch.

Thirteen

IN THE WEEKS that followed, I saw Jeff and Ena only
once or twice. Jeff looked just like his father—tall,
dark, well-built. Ena was fair, with long, light brown
hair, and a slender model's figure. Neither one of
them said much. Ena usually had business over the
phone, and Jeff kept a polite distance. Though they
were busy house hunting, they managed to make
their presence known at Aunt Dee's in various ways.

Every week there were changes. One day I arrived to find the heavy juniper bushes in the front ripped out. The next week, new sod had been laid, and a border of impatience bloomed under the olive tree. Then the old wrought iron fence around the drive was replaced by a neatly built, one-foot-high brick wall.

"He does things I don't even need," Aunt Dee commented one morning. "But it looks nice, don't you think? I hated those dark bushes. I wanted Harry to get rid of them a long time ago, but he never found time. Jeff just does things because he wants me to be happy."

I hoped so, but I couldn't really get a feel for him or Ena. They were never around long enough. Ena had a strong, bubbly energy but didn't channel any in my direction. Of course, why should she? She'd never met me before now. And Jeff kept a mysterious aloofness. He wasn't like Gina—open, curious about what I was doing with their mother. Jeff remained watchful, from a distance. According to Aunt Dee, he couldn't see any value in telling painful stories. Also, he didn't believe in his sister's medical-alternative, homeopathy. Still, he couldn't deny that his mother appeared happier and healthier, and thankfully, he didn't interfere with our meetings.

By October the weather was still warmish, but the winds crept in early, not bothering to wait for Halloween, when the Santa Ana's often kicked up.

"I've painted another painting," Aunt Dee announced.

Usually she waited for me to notice, but this time she showed an eagerness for my impression. We walked into the living room, the dogs eyeing me but no longer barking.

She'd hung the painting, unframed, over the china cabinet. On a canvas larger than any she'd used so far, an unmistakable landscape of Indonesia spread in soft blue and green tones. Thin, white clouds dusted the sky. No sign of stormy weather, as in other paintings. In the distance a volcano loomed half-hidden in clouds. Two people worked the land in the foreground, the flooded paddies held water that was calm and clear as a mirror. Off to one side, a path bordered by flowers led to a grass shelter, nestled between coconut palms.

I could hardly believe my eyes. She had distanced herself from the masculine mountains, calmed her subconscious with the gentle, flooded paddies, and added life, people.

"It's Indonesia," Aunt Dee openly admitted. She pointed to the two figures. "He's a workaholic, and she's telling him she's going home now."

We laughed, but I sensed the depths of her words. The painting was the best she'd done. It had feeling. It had meaning. It showed healing, and I had to wipe the tears from the corners of my eyes. Indonesia, the word and the place, no longer needed to be forbidden.

NOVEMBER AND DECEMBER brought a little rain. Just a sprinkle here and there, but nothing of the torrential downpours that were predicted because of El Niño. People were beginning to believe El Niño was a myth. The temperatures were not cold, and a light sweater was enough. But I could sense a difference in the air, a hint of change.

For Aunt Dee, the change started with Jeff and Ena finding their new home and moving out in mid-December. The news surprised me. I'd half-expected them to stay much longer, or perhaps buy a bigger house and move their mother in with them. But they did neither. On a rainy weekend, just before Christmas, they moved into their own home, a few miles away, and left Aunt Dee with her space—and left me thinking that perhaps I'd misjudged them.

For me, the change came with the holidays and the sudden hubbub brought on by my three children and a daughter-in-law being home for Christmas. My routine became nonexistent, but nights, when the kids thought us "old fogies" had gone to bed, I took the opportunity to sort out my aunt's stories, and my thoughts, and read through the literature of rheumatoid arthritis.

And then before I knew it, January second rolled around, all the kids were back in their own lives, and I could return to my own schedule. The first person I called was Aunt Dee.

"How are you?" I asked.

"Fine."

"I've stopped my methotrexate," she said.

"What? Completely?"

"Yes."

"How do you feel?"

"Fine. I never want to take it again."

"Have you told your doctor?"

"Yes. He said it would be okay for a while."

I realized that her decision made me question my own beliefs. It scared me to think that I might have had something to do with her discontinuing a medication that by Western standards helped relieve the symptoms of rheumatoid arthritis. Did I believe strongly enough in my own treatments, in Gina's homeopathy, to experiment on my aunt?

"When did you go off?"

"Just before Christmas."

Too soon for any setbacks. If she were strong enough, surely there couldn't be any harm in seeing what would happen. She could always go back on the medication. I was ashamed of my own lack of conviction.

"I just got off the phone with your mother," Aunt Dee said. "She told me you were taking her to see Lieke. Could I come? I haven't seen her since her stroke."

My mother's younger sister, Lieke, had suffered a massive stroke just before Uncle Harry's death. It had not paralyzed her but had left her confused in many ways. Incredibly, she could remember teachers she'd had in elementary school, old friends, and the horrors of war, but what she had done that morning was lost in the short-term cavities of her brain. She also had to relearn how to walk, how to use the phone, even how to eat.

"Sure," I told Aunt Dee. "I'll pick you up Thursday morning at ten."

We planned for Gina to join us and make it a family outing. My Aunt Lieke would be pleasantly surprised. She cried frequently on the phone to my mother that she was bored, and that no one visited her.

But Thursday morning dawned with heavy rain clouds, the forecast ominous. Gina canceled because a skunk or opossum had gotten stuck under her house, and exterminators were coming to remove it. I called my mother and asked if she still wanted to go. Maybe this was the beginning of El Niño. We didn't want to get swept away.

"How do you feel about driving in the rain?" my mother asked.

"I have good brakes and new windshield wipers."

"Then I want to go. I haven't seen my sister for two weeks and she's upset. She's having a bad hair day or something. Can you bring a good pair of scissors in case we have to cut her hair a little? You know how she gets agitated."

I did know. It was part of her personality since the stroke. Lots of things set her off, not being able to put her pants on right, not remembering how to make hot chocolate, not being able to take a walk for fear she wouldn't find her way back. These traumas were usually resolved by a visit, and discussing old times.

I called Aunt Dee, knowing she didn't go out in the rain. The cold and wet aggravated her arthritis. She told me she usually bundles up and stays in the house on rainy days.

"Don't worry," I told her. "You can join us the next time we go."

"Well, I'm really all dressed," she said, her voice soft and unsure. She sounded disappointed, like a child who'd been told she couldn't go on a trip.

"You still want to come?" I asked.

She hesitated. "Yes."

"I'll be there at ten, then." I called my mother back. She was equally surprised.

When mother and I arrived, Aunt Dee must have been watching for us. She came out the instant we drove up. Wearing a tailored gray pantsuit and heavy socks in sandals, she marched out to us apparently unperturbed by the weather.

The clouds had not yet unleashed the promised downpour, but a cold mist pervaded. Aunt Dee handed my mother a small bag of kumquats.

"You can make jam from them."

"Ah, good idea," my mother said, taking the bag. "Usually I cut them and mix them with hot chili peppers."

Aunt Dee nodded. "I like to eat that with rice, but I have to be careful. Too much spice is not good for me. She held open a plastic bag from the supermarket. "I brought some grapefruit for Lieke."

"Let's put some of your tangerines in too."

My mother, a spry seventy-five-year-old, stepped up on the new one-foot wall and picked a few low-hanging fruits.

"Let me do it, Mom." I had already been through two broken legs with her—at the same time—an accident she'd sustained while shopping a few years ago. "Okay, that's enough," I said, after picking a half-dozen. "We better get going."

Mother and Aunt Dee argued politely, each of them offering to sit in the backseat of my two-door Integra. Mother won. She squeezed into the back, Aunt Dee sat up front, I closed the door, and off we went.

The rain began as we drove over the pass and along Pacific Coast Highway to the Malibu trailer park where my Aunt Lieke lived with her friend Piet. Tiny drops at first, then larger and heavier ones. The ocean loomed on our left, gray and stormy,, the horizon indistinct.

In the rearview mirror I could see my mother frowning. She didn't like driving in bad weather. Aunt Dee had her eyes on the road as well.

"Everyone okay?" I asked.

"Yes," they both piped up with optimistic voices.

I laughed to myself. Neither one of them would choose to drive in this weather, but I could deliver to them this simple joy—the safe drive to a dear family member in need. It made me feel good inside.

By the time we arrived at the trailer park, the rain was slow but steady. We made a dash for the trailer, me holding an umbrella over my mother and aunt while raindrops trickled down the back of my neck.

Aunt Lieke came out onto the covered porch wearing the smile of an overeager child.

"You're here," she said, hugging us in turn. "Come in, come in. You haven't seen my new home. It's big. It's beautiful."

Piet's son had recently arranged for his father and Aunt Lieke to live in the trailer. Neither were candidates for a nursing home, but they needed some supervision, between Aunt Lieke's helplessness, and Piet's prostate cancer and severe asthma, requiring an oxygen tank. At the trailer park, they were a few minutes away from Piet's son and family, and the nearby university offered "meals on wheels," all of which made for a relatively protected environment.

Aunt Lieke showed us around the trailer. I could feel Aunt Dee taking everything in. There was nothing homey about the place. No pretty things, no paintings. Just a chair, a couch, a table, beds in the bedrooms, water-spattered mirrors in the bathroom. It feel like a real home.

We sat and had coffee from cracked mugs that I remembered from my childhood—white with cherry, orange, and plum faces. The donut holes I brought, we ate from the box, unlike the pretty dishes Aunt Dee always served on. Napkins were paper towels. Sugar and milk came from their cartons.

Sitting at the "dining" card table, we could see into the kitchen. While Piet chatted away, sucking in deep breaths of air between words, I observed Aunt

Lieke as she went into the kitchen to get a drink of water. She filled her glass from the sink, but Piet interrupted his chatter to tell her he had cold water in the refrigerator.

"Oh, yes," Lieke said. "That would be better." She grinned, poured the tap water out of her glass, moved the faucet from one side of the sink to the other, then refilled the glass from the tap and drank it.

Aunt Dee, my mother, and I exchanged glances. I could feel my mother's fearful concern for her sister, and Aunt Dee's sympathy. We didn't say anything, and Piet just grunted.

"My hair is a mess. I hate it," Aunt Lieke said, as she rejoined us. "And every time I get it done, the girl charges me . . ." she paused, thinking. "A lot of money and it looks the same—awful."

"We'll fix it," Aunt Dee said, getting up from the table.

"Excuse us for a while, Piet," my mother said.

"Ya, ya." He coughed, and waved us out of the room. He went back to sit in the chair where he'd been potting a plant. I saw Aunt Dee look at the dirt that fell to the shag carpet. She and I exchanged another sympathetic look, then followed Lieke to her bathroom, where we placed her on a folding chair in front of the mirror.

Mother took up the post of observer, and Aunt Dee spray-wet Lieke's hair and began to comb it into her face. I cut, under Aunt Dee's instruction, with Mother chiming in now and then about maybe a little more on the left, a little shorter in the back. We cut and snipped, and when we finished, even I was surprised at how good it looked.

We went back to our coffee and tea and let Aunt

Lieke talk about old times and complain about her children who never came to see her. Then it was back into the rain, and home through the foggy canyon.

TWO DAYS LATER Gina called me.

"I can't believe my mother went out in the rain."

"Is she okay?" I asked, thinking that perhaps Aunt Dee had had a flare up, and Gina was going to reprimand me.

"She's great! In fact she wanted to get her hair done, and when I told her I couldn't get over there in the evening, she drove over herself. She never drives in the dark."

"She drove to your house in the dark?"

"Yes!"

Zincite

Tall jagged cliffs
warm ocean waves
Zincite crystals
flower fragrances
chocolate cake
and angel voices,
all layers
of sensuality
that synthesize power, energy, and creativity
to stimulate
the currents
blocked for so long.

Fourteen

WITH FEBRUARY CAME the rain, the real El Niño rain. For days we didn't see the sun. Streets flooded, houses leaked, and heating bills went up.

Aunt Dee had trouble sleeping. Pain bothered her, but she only took salicylates. She still refused the methotrexate her doctor encouraged her to resume.

Gina treated her with different homeopathic dilutions. I asked her if she was bothered by the anniver-
sary of Uncle Harry's death.

"Forty-one years we were together," she said. "Of
course I'm sad. I was so used to him, but there are
times when it is easier. I don't have to do anything,
and I don't have to try to please anyone now." Her
eyes were clear and thoughtful. "You know, all my
life I felt I had to look busy. In the camp, I looked
busy to keep peering eyes off me. At Aunt Erika's, I
kept busy so she wouldn't think I was lazy. Even in
my marriage, I felt I had to stay busy. If I heard Harry
coming into the house, I hurriedly made sure I was
doing something, anything. Now I can just be myself
and do what I need to do for me when I want to do
it. And when I don't want to do anything, I don't."
She smiled. "But that's not very often."

Her voice, though tentative, had new strength.
I'm not sure she recognized it yet, but there were
signs of her emerging self. She was no longer afraid
to drive herself to evening Bible study classes, and
her latest painting suggested a transition within the
psyche. In vivid colors, she explored the ocean
depths. Three dolphins, bright coral, small fish swimming in clear, calm waters. The jagged rocks were in
the background now, still a part of her, but smaller, no
longer holding her prisoner, and contained in a bril-
liant sky.

As March moved in, and the rain subsided a bit,
Aunt Dee's rheumatologist felt she had been off
the methotrexate long enough. But she still
refused to take it, telling him that for the last two
months she had never felt stronger. Yes, she'd had
pain, but at least she could go shopping for more

than ten minutes without having to hang onto her grocery cart. She woke up more easily, and went to bed happier.

To prove that she knew what she was talking about, she'd showed the doctor the pharmaceutical list of methotrexate side effects, many of which she'd experienced. But rather than being sympathetic, her doctor had become angry with the pharmacist who must have given her the information. The information came in the mail, Aunt Dee had explained. And why shouldn't she know the side effects? It was her body.

The doctor warned her that if she didn't go back on the methotrexate now, it would be too late. She'd get worse, and then medication wouldn't help her. Aunt Dee refused to believe him and left the doctor's office holding her ground.

When she got home, Jeff and Ena happened by, and, no doubt needing some reassurance, she proudly told them of her experience at the doctor's office. But Jeff wasn't pleased. He berated his mother for only listening to Gina, and by the time he and Ena left, old doubts had crept in. Aunt Dee felt unsteady on her feet. The room began to spin. She called Gina, who rushed over to give her something to make her more comfortable and to stop the dizziness. But it didn't stop her spinning on the inside.

That evening, she called me

"Are you still dizzy?" I asked.

"Only a little."

"Other than that, how do you feel?"

"Good," she said, drawing the word out.

I could hear her uncertainty and doubt, her fear that she might be doing something wrong. The fear that her son would disapprove of her, that he some-how wouldn't love her. She wanted me to tell her, everything was going to be alright. But I couldn't do that. I honestly didn't know. I could only believe in what I preached, and I could call Jeff.

"Wait a day or two," I said. "See if the dizziness passes. Perhaps it was brought on by stress. You took a bold stand with the doctor and with Jeff."

"Yes, I was very nervous."

"Then listen to your body. Really listen to it. And listen to the voice inside you. You'll know if you have to go back on medication."

I heard her sigh of relief.

"Okay," she said.

I PREPARED TO give Jeff a good talking-to. Why couldn't he just support his mother? But before I could call him, he called me.

"I'm worried about my mother," he said. "I don't know what she's doing. I don't trust doctors a hun-dred percent either, but I'm skeptical of my sister. Maybe you could tell me what's going on?"

I felt my body tighten. "Jeff, your mother needs to feel secure in making her own decisions. For the first time in her life she is doing things her way." I emphasized, *her way*. "You don't need to . . ." I searched for the right words. "Take care of her."

"What exactly are you saying?" He spoke slowly. I could almost see his neck veins bulging.

"She doesn't need you to take over where your father left off," I said bluntly.

I heard him breathing on the other end, gather-ing his thoughts. I got ready for his anger. Aunt Dee said she was always afraid to tell him anything because he might react like his father.

"I would never take over her life," Jeff said. He sounded calm, almost sad. "I've purposely left Gina to handle all the emotional and personal issues, while I looked after Mom's finances and any physical repairs needed around the house. I just want to know what's going on. She and Gina don't tell me anything and I worry about her too."

"Maybe they don't tell you anything because they're afraid you'll yell at them or get upset like your dad."

"I wouldn't do that. I hated it when my dad yelled at me. And he did it often. He'd get upset about something or another, my grades, my friends, something. He'd yell, slam his hand on the table, but I never said anything. There was no use in saying anything, but my face would begin to twitch. Then he'd tell me to stop twitching, which made my face twitch worse. I still do it when I get upset."

This was not what I had expected. His voice sounded sincere, and I even detected a hint of his own pain as it related to his family. Since I knew that Aunt Dee intended Gina and Jeff to hear her story, I decided, now was a good time to let Jeff in on some of the traumas his mother had endured. Traumas that could help him understand some of her idiosyncrasies. I talked for a long time.

He listened.

Of course, he never knew about the rape, but he also didn't know about Aunt Erika's dog, or that air conditioning aggravated her arthritis. He didn't know that Gina had warned their father about his heart, or that his father had been emotionally abusive toward his mother.

There was a long silence after I finished.

"Maybe she doesn't tell me anything because I'm a man," he said.

I suddenly saw another side to the picture. Aunt Dee hadn't said Jeff got upset and angry. She said she was afraid he might get upset and angry like Harry. "Jeff, give her some time. She's going through a real change in her life. She's getting to know who she is for the first time."

We ended our conversation on good terms, and I sat back to absorb a new realization. It had to do with truths and perceptions, and how old ways of thinking and unhealed scars can distort the meaning of a situation.

BY THE NEXT day, Aunt Dee's dizziness had cleared, and two weeks later when I visited, she appeared to be glowing with a new energy. It couldn't be the weather, for even though we were approaching April, spring had not arrived. El Niño apparently intended to keep us damp and cool.

"How do you feel?" I asked.

"Oh, a little pain here and there. You know. It's never really gone. But I've started physical therapy once a week, and it seems to help. I feel stronger. And, oh, I met a charming woman the other day in Bible studies. She's from Indonesia, visiting her married daughter here."

The two of them talked and shared stories of their common birthplace. Aunt Dee invited the woman for dinner, and the woman invited Aunt Dee to stay with her if she ever came to Indonesia.

"Would you go?"

Aunt Dee shrugged, one of those shy smiles playing over her lips.

"Maybe," she said.

"Really?"

"I think I'm strong enough now, but we'll have to see, I may be busy. I have other news." She paused for suspense. "Jeff and Ena are going to have a baby."

A baby. How absolutely perfect. Free at last, Aunt Dee would have another chance to be the grandmother she'd always wanted to be.

"God is good," she said. "A baby. There's going to be a new baby."

"Life is good," I answered.

"Yes," she said, and her eyes sparkled and danced with life, sensual as any flower in bloom, bright as any crystal.

Afterword

July 1998

AFTER MONTHS OF working with her, and furiously typing my notes in the evening, I presented Aunt Dee with a manuscript of her stories. She took the pages gratefully, but I did not hear back from her for several weeks.

Finally, she called.

"I'm sorry it took me so long to read the book," she said. "I'd read a few pages and break down in tears. I cried and cried. Sometimes I couldn't stop."

Changes began happening quickly after Aunt Dee read her life in story form. The manuscript made its rounds to Gina and Jeff. They too cried, for they had never known their mother in this way. Now they understood why she was who she was, and did the things she did: her immaculate house, her fear of dogs, her need for love. Her childrens' acceptance gave Aunt Dee new strength. She joined the local

128 YMCA. Started swimming lessons and classes in t'ai chi. She gardens, walks, continues to paint, has no trouble driving in the dark or going out in inclement weather.

Pain? Yes, of course she still has days when the pain bothers her, days when she's worked too hard in the garden, walked too much, lifted too heavy a grocery bag. She has good days and bad days, just like the rest of us, but she doesn't have the nightmares. Those are captured in the stories, locked on the pages of this book.

I doubt that this telling of stories can reverse her illness and make normal the deformities of her hands and feet, but by some strange coincidence, a few arthritic nodules on her hands have diminished. Her fingers are warm and no longer red, the veins in her feet no longer protrude grossly, and she has successfully weaned herself off all allopathic medication.

She walks in different shoes, open, less constricting. They fit and are comfortable, as she is in her . new life.

Bibliography

Ananth, Jambur, M.D., D.P.M., F.R.C.P. (Canada) "Musculoskeletal Disorders and Rheumatoid Arthritis." *Comprehensive Textbook of Psychiatry/VI,* Sixth Ed. Vol. 2 . 1538-1544. Baltimore, MD: Williams & Wilkins, 1995

Downe-Womboldt, Barbara L., Melanson, Patricia M. "Emotions, Coping, and Psychological Well-Being in Elderly People With Arthritis." *Western Journal of Nursing Research* 17(3)1995: 250-65.

Estés, Clarissa Pinkola, Ph.D. "Vasalisa and the Baba Yaga." *Theater of the Imagination,* Tape three, set one. Sounds True Tapes, 1997.

Frawley, David, Dr. Ayurvedic *Healing for Health Care and Professionals.* Book IV. 37. American Institute of Vedic Studies, New Mexico, 1996.

References

Homeopathy
Ayurveda
Dr. Subrata Kumar Banerjea
169-B Bowbazaar St.
Calcutta, India 700-012

Overseas advisor and visiting lecturer: Atlantic Academy of Classical Homoeopathy (New York, USA); South Australian & Victorian College of Classical Homoeopathy (Adelaide & Melbourne, Australia); Fellow of the Akademie Homoopathischer Deutscher Zenralverein (Germany); Fellow of the Academy of Natural Medicine (Essex, England).

Homeopathy
Ayurveda
Herbs, Aromatherapy
Gina V. Tyler, D.I.HOM.
 5354 Don Pio Dr.
Woodland Hills, CA 91364
Kinesiology
(818) 887-2243

Ayurvedic Medicine
Panchakarma
Ayurvedic Health Center
17308 W. Sunset Blvd.
Pacific Palisades, CA
(310) 454-5531